I0134574

MY OWN LITTLE CORNER

By

Annemarie Brown

These are true stories. I was born in
Amsterdam before World War II. My father had
lost his right arm when he was 17 years old.
My mother married him against her father's
advice and since you needed parental
permission until the age of 25, I was
conceived prior to their marriage.

I was a mean child. At least that is
what they said. But I did fight and work hard
for what I thought was right and fair. They
also said that I was "my Dad's right arm"
because I was allowed to help him with
everything.

I want you to know that during the war
and thereafter I was never hungry, was always
clothed, and was a content and happy child
most of the time.

I don't want you to feel sorry for me,
but teach your children right from wrong, that

people should be allowed different opinions,
and that they don't have to agree with
everything they are told.

CHAPTER 1

A SINFUL SONG

The morning was foggy and misty, nothing
unusual for Amsterdam. I remember turning the
fruit a quarter turn. Going between the row
of fruit on my hands and knees turning apples,
pears, potatoes, and eggs was my morning job.
Since I was small there could be more rows on
the living room floor.

     The doorbell rang, although we did not
expect anyone and we had heard no one coming.
Mam opened the door and there were two tall SS
officers. They did not wait to be invited in.
They pushed my mother aside and turned facing
her in the entry hall.

     They wanted Pap! My mother ordered me to
go across the street to Mrs. Mendes. She only
told me to do this when there were things
going on that I was not supposed to hear or

see. I passed the two tall men who were still standing in the hallway. "Hello, little girl, how are you?" "Very well, thank you," I said. "What is your name?" "Ansje," I answered.

I knew the next question just as well as I knew the previous ones. I also knew exactly what to answer. "How old are you?" "I am five years old, but almost six," was my answer.

And then came the dangerous one that had taken hours of practice to answer. I was taught to go into the "I don't know" mode or the "I don't remember" mode. "Where is your father, you know, your Papa? Is he with your uncle? And where is your uncle?" "I don't know. I don't think I have an uncle!" My mother interrupted by sending me across the street.

Every morning and evening we had practiced questions and answers. Somehow I knew I better do as I was told. Mam said lives depended on answers and sometimes silence was even more important.

I went across the street, but as I reached the steps going up to Mrs. Mendes' house, I heard our front door close hard. I turned around and saw the two SS officers lead my Dad away, one holding his arm with a hand on one side and on the other side the man had a hand on Pap's shoulder pushing him forward.

I sat down on the steps and watched them walk away down the street. I wondered what Pap had done this time for them to pick him up again.

My stomach felt funny, but I did not cry. I had also learned that in our rehearsals. My mother came walking quickly across the street carrying my sister in her arms. She was nervous every time Pap was picked up for something.

She was surprised to see me sitting halfway up the step, and the surprise quickly turned to anger. She always became very angry when I did not do exactly what she told me to do because it could mean the difference between life and death for me, or any of us for that matter.

Mrs. Mendes had come down when she had heard my mother yelling at me. They talked for a few minutes, keeping their voices low, and then we went home. As the front door securely locked behind us, I was again

reminded to do what I was told, and for the
millionth time we went through a practice
session. If I needed more practice she was to
accommodate me, and that meant two or three
hours of drilling questions and answers, which
I was totally sick of.

As my mother tended to my sister, I sat
on the arm of the big chair in the living
room, which was kind of a safe corner, close
to the potbelly stove. It kept the room
comfortable with only one scoop of briquettes.

When I smelled bacon it was dinner time.
All the drapes were closed and the towels and
pieces of blanket securely placed in the
window sills to keep the smell in. The
neighbors must not smell what we had to eat.
My mother did not want them begging at the
door.

Pap came back the next day. The Germans
had picked him up because someone had seen us
watch the soldiers parade and I had been
singing the song with the marching soldiers!
They had asked him why he had taught his child
German marching songs. They threatened to
send him to Germany. They threatened him with
hard labor. He really did not know how I had

learned the melody so fast and he could not
imagine how I had learned the words! They
told him they would shoot him without another
warning if they should catch him watching
another marching parade.

I still remember that song today. When I
sing it or just hum the melody, I see them
walk away with Pap. The only thing that
puzzles me is that I know the words in Dutch
and not in German. Did Pap teach me the words
after all?

He really did not. I learned that song
by watching them march by only one time. It
is very easy to sing and easy to walk to. I
proved later to be very musical, and have very
good rhythm.

This is how the song goes:
Zeg meisje lief, heb jij vanavond vry?
Heili, Heilo.
Dan maak ik gauw van jou
Een goed soldaten vrouw,
Heili, heili, heilo, heili, heilo.

(Hey cute little girl, are you available
tonight?
Heili, heilo.

I'll quickly turn you into a good
soldier's wife.)

CHAPTER 2

SOUP FOR NETTY

My regular morning drill had paid off time after time. One Monday morning I began to realize how important my morning speech and answer game had become. My aunt Dina, Pap's sister-in-law (married to his oldest brother, Peter) came to visit with my cousin Netty. Pap and I had been to her house before, but this was the first time she came to our house.

They lived approximately 12 long blocks away in the Albert Kuip Street on the third floor. It had a small front door with three doorbells instead of four. The downstairs floor was a shop. I never figured out what they sold there because the front window was painted white almost all the way up to the top of the window. The stairs were narrow and spiraled up, each floor landing getting smaller and smaller.

The only benefit the top floor had was a small window in the opposite wall from the door. A few years later, that window made it possible for me to escape from a horrible individual who followed me after school.

The next street over, just in front of the main street Ferdinand Bol Street, had my favorite ice cream store where I used to stop on the way back from high school.

On Monday morning my mother put the dining room table in the living room. I thought maybe we needed more room for supplies, but that proved to be wrong. I was already spending enough time every morning tending to fruit and eggs! But like always Mam never did anything without a good reason and calculated every step of the way in advance.

Pap was walking around nervously all morning when finally around 11 A.M. (I remember it was early for lunch) my aunt and cousin came over again. She greeted Mam and Pap, made a fuss over my little sister, and right away Aunt Dina and Netty sat down at that newly placed table in the living room. I sat at the table opposite my aunt, and my

cousin sat to my right at the end of the table
with her back to the door.

I wondered why they had been here all of
10 minutes and neither had inquired about my
uncle who was hiding in our small basement!
This was their husband and father! I valued
my hide well enough to keep my mouth shut. I
was never to speak first, not to suggest or
even assume anything. Although I assumed
silently that neither one of them knew that
Uncle Peter was hiding below right under their
feet. Then I heard a usual comment directed
to me. "You are so serious and so silent.
How have you been?" "Fine, thank you," I
said.

To relatives and acquaintances I was to
use the same well rehearsed language and
facial expressions. One of Mam's lines was
"No one is to be trusted; family and friends
are the worst! Sometimes life may depend upon
it."

Mam brought a bowl of soup and a slice of
bread for each one of them. They ate fast and
eagerly. I knew they had not eaten for
several days. My aunt's brief visit the day
before had been to ask for food. Mam never

gave food to take but sometimes she would
allow some people to eat at our house. That
was always dangerous, and that proved to be
true again.

My aunt finished her food and went to the
kitchen to ask for more, but I already knew
Mam would refuse. After not eating for many
days you cannot eat a lot all at once.
Vomiting was the usual result, and that was a
waste.

As Netty was finishing her last piece of
bread, there was a loud rumble. Someone was
loudly banging on the front door with two
fists. I had heard that noise before, so I
watched the horror reaction on my cousin's
face.

I did not react. I was taught to stay
calm. Jannette was more than a year older
than I but had not had the morning drills and
preparation.

Either Mam or Pap opened the door and the
familiar squeak warned everyone (even in the
basement) that someone had come in. With one
or two big steps two large, tall S.S. officers
were in the middle of our entry hall. I could
not see through the door, but I had seen it

many times before. One entered the room where
my cousins and I were still sitting at the
table. The officer took off his hat and sat
down on the chair where my aunt had been just
a few minutes before.

"Hello, girls." "Hello," said Netty. I
did not answer because I was not supposed to.
I just looked straight at him, trying not to
be afraid. I folded my hands which gave me
strength. To feel one hand squeeze the other
or pull the other made me feel strong and
aware. He directed the same question at me.
"Fine," I said. The routine drill was now in
progress. "Do you live here?" My cousin
answered, "No, I came to eat here." "Are you
still hungry?" "No," she said. "My aunt gave
me enough."

"Is your mother here?" "Yes," she said.
Then he turned to me. "You live here don't
you?" "Yes, Sir." Two words and direct eye
contact. It is amazing that a five-year-old
does not crumble, but that shows you what can
be taught to a child and maintained with
enough scare tactics.

Then came the usual, again, "You look so
serious. Are you angry or unhappy? "Then came

the usual again: "You look so serious, are you angry or unhappy"? We just came to visit. But by the way.......(watch out!, I thought here it comes) he directed his question to Netty, "Where is your Dad, did he come with you? "I don't know " Netty said I don't know where my Daddy is."

I looked at her and realized it was a good thing she did not know. She was ready to blow. I heard her blabber on, that she had not seen him...she had not been to this house before...her mother brought her here to eat a meal because they were hungry.

Then he directed the question to me: "Did she come to see her Dad?" Someone, a neighbor, had said that he was seen here with us. I looked directly at him and said, "I don't know her father. This is the first time she and her Mam came to visit." This tall, mean looking big man made his eyes look right through me, but my mother had promised me that he could not see what I was thinking even if he said he could.

He took Netty by the hand and led her into the entry hall. As he closed the door behind him my heart started pounding, but I

had learned how to handle the fear. I took a
deep breath, put my arms up high, and
pretended I was showing my Dad how tall I was.
I heard in the back of my mind "How tall are
you Ansje?" "This tall, Pap," and my body was
under control!

They all left - my aunt and cousin, and
the S.S., and Mam and Pap did not say one word
about what happened or my uncle in the
basement. The officers had searched the house
for hidden radios and hand grenades, but of
course found nothing. My uncle Peter was not
the first person hiding in the basement, and
he would not be the last.

I did not see my aunt or cousin again for
months, and it was obvious to me that neither
of them, not even my aunt, knew my uncle (her
husband) was with us.

CHAPTER 3

THE SHEEP

"Aunt Jopie is coming," my mother had said. My mother had an errand to run. "If she gets here before I return, let her in, but remember how to watch her."

There was an oval washtub, the size of a horse water trough, which was 3\4 filled with wheat kernels. Another tub like it was standing outside which was used for our bathtub. The tub with wheat was considered a tub of gold, since 90% of the people were on a ration of one potato each every other day.

I was sitting on the arm of the big chair, which I called my little corner, when there was a knock at the door. I had to stretch to undo the top lock; the lower one and the knob were easy. Aunt Jopie greeted me over friendly like most people in those days: I felt it was just to impress my parents.

She had just married my Dad's youngest brother Henk, who had off and on been our basement guest. She was a pleasant person, skinny and pretty.

Even though she acted very calm, I could see the stress in her face and eyes. She took a long look at the wheat and pointed at it but before she could open her mouth. I jumped in front of her and said, "My mother does not want you to touch that. She will feed you when she gets home." She was slightly irritated because of my abrupt loud instruction and she must have noticed my perfect lines. Maybe she knew they were rehearsed. She probably did not know my butt would be black and blue if I would let her take something, especially that wheat.

That wheat had become a mental and physical problem to me, and it was her husband who had been the cause of the severe punishment I had suffered over that wheat.

Just a few weeks earlier I had been put in charge of my sister, while my mother went to deliver a radio. My uncle Henk had come over and had stolen a bag of wheat while I played hide and go seek with my sister. My uncle had managed to distract me. I was told to keep an eye on my sister but to also keep an eye on that wheat at all times.

When my uncle joined the game he hid my sister for me to find her. I forgot about the wheat. I went to look for her, which gave him enough time to take a bag full.

I never figured out how my mother knew that there was any gone. I could not see that the top she had smoothed out had been disturbed. My mother yelled at me that I was irresponsible, that she could not depend on me when it really counted, that from now on to not let anyone in the house. She reminded me how right she was that family was not to be trusted at anytime.

I woke up the next morning with swollen eyes from crying. I did not cry often; it was a sign of losing control and I needed to learn to not lose control. I needed to learn to not trust, to give out no information, and to not feel sorry for anyone. We, us - Mam, Pap, my sister and I - had to come first and everyone else later when it would be Mam or Pap's choice, certainly not the choice for a snotnose like me!

After that drastic affair I sure watched that wheat and protected it when I was told. The black and blue marks on my body reminded me physically for days and visually for weeks.

This time, I did not have my sister to worry about, so I walked ahead of my Aunt Jopie into the dining room, making sure she followed me. She asked if I could give her something to eat. I told her she had to wait until Mam got home.

If she only knew that a few feet behind her in the linen closet there were three large whole cheeses nicely covered with sheets and towels. If you opened the door you could see nothing special, just a regular linen closet. Behind the front rows of towels there was also bacon, and on the right top shelf the key to that closet door.

The keys were only used when everyone was gone, and it was usually Mam who was the last to leave.

I could not look at the door because that would draw suspicion, and, besides, I was to look at the people at all times. So I looked at her.

She talked to me and called me "a little girl, with wise eyes and a smart mouth." "Thanks a lot, Lady. That is not what Pap thinks!" Her comments did not bother me as long as she stayed away from that wheat. While looking at her, I could see the cheeses in my mind in the closet, the wheat in the tub in the hallway, and behind the sliding wooden doors the fruit and eggs on the floor. I had just turned them a 1/4 turn this morning. I heard a noise. Did she know her husband was here? Was Mam home yet? I could not leave her to go see, so when the door opened and my mother greeted her, I was relieved.

I knew my mother would not thank me in front of my Aunt for doing a good job watching the food, especially the wheat. But when everyone was gone, I would sit on the arm of the easy chair and she would tell me how proud she was of me. She told me that if I helped like that we would make it through these hard times. But this was not the best reward. The best reward came when I was walking down the street with Pap and he would tell me that he was so proud of me that I helped Mam when he was not home and how smart I was for such a little girl. He always squeezed my hand while we were walking together. That gave me security and I promised to be the best I could be.

Pap liked to practice what he learned in school and he would explain to me how he could tell what people had wrong with them by the way they walked.

"See that lady over there? What can you tell me about her?" The lady was walking in front of us so we were watching her from behind. I watched closely and could see she was heavier than my mother and swinging slightly from side to side. When she crossed the street Pap said, "Look, she is pregnant."

From a very early age I was learning to watch body movement of people. It gave me a good feeling that he would think I could be part of his real studies, so I started watching people in a very special way.

I was watching my aunt's eyes when her husband and my Dad came in! I knew something special was up. These four people had never been together as far as I could remember. I turned the coffee grinder handle to grind wheat to make bread, while Mam made hot water for tea. She went under the house for some butter and while we were eating my uncle suggested they send me to another room to play.

Pap told them that I was safer and more secure than many adults and gave me that look of pride. He knew he had made me feel good.

As they went on talking, I could not believe my ears! The planning and arguing went fast and furious. All I really understood was that Pap had found sheep in a small pasture and he had watched them hours at a time for several days. The same two sheep had strayed twice at almost the same time of the day to the far end of the small pasture.

They got a knife (Mam's large butcher knife), a rope, gunny sack and some other things and put it on the back of Pap's bicycle, and Pap and his brother Henk left.

As Pap walked out the door handling that heavy bicycle with one hand he looked back and said, "Take care of your Mother, Ans." I often wondered what he really meant by that (to take care of my mother). He always said that when he went on a trip or job: thus far he had always come back, or maybe it was just a way of saying goodbye with a special meaning.

I always promised to be strong no matter what. The rear tire of the bicycle bounced down the three front steps and off they went.

I was allowed to get one egg and Mam boiled it, so the yolk was still soft. Left alone with my bread and egg, which was my favorite food, I sat on the arm of the big chair, and I felt content.

As time went by and darkness came, my aunt was crying. My mother tried to comfort her, but I had seen her eyes before. She was already scared when she came in earlier that day and now she was getting frantic.

Mam and Aunt Jopie were considering what could have gone wrong. Maybe the sheep had not separated from the small herd. Maybe they got caught on the way home. No one was allowed on the streets after dark and there was a soldier on every corner of every street. My mother helped me get ready for bed, my sister had been asleep for some time.

I was used to Pap not coming home right away and seldom on the day he promised, and I somehow knew my patience would pay off: it always had before. I had heard of other fathers and even mothers not coming home, but that did not apply to me. At least that was a safe assumption.

I was still awake when I heard Pap coming home. No one talked, not even whispered. I could hardly tell how many feet were coming in.

I shot up out of bed and ran into the entry hall. There was Pap covered with blood from head to toe! Mam took over his bicycle and brought it further into the hall. When everyone was in the closet the door was locked. No one turned the light on. That was not permitted after dark. Pap pointed at the gunny sack on the bike and his eyes caught mine. He winked and I knew than he was all right. The blood wasn't his; it was from the sheep he had caught and slaughtered.

My mother checked the drapes and towels to make sure the smell could not escape the house. Some of the gunny sacks were put in the coal shed, one in the basement, and one was left in the kitchen.

Mam helped Pap take off the bloody clothes and put them in salt water. This way the smell would not stay in the clothes. She put the bucket under the sink and started cutting open the gunny sack that had been put in the kitchen.

It is amazing how handy they had become working in the dark. Everything was done silently and speedily.

Pap said that tomorrow I would eat mutton. Sheep is the only T.B free animal so we should be safe.

When I woke up the next morning my aunt and uncle were gone. All the blood was gone. Pap was wearing the same clothes again without a trace of blood on them. The gunny sacks were gone. In fact it looked like the event of the night had never happened. Mam made my favorite egg for breakfast and Pap watched me eat bite for bite, smiling contentedly.

We sat by the potbelly stove and while Mam was feeding the baby Pap told me the story of the night before.

"Henk only gets a small portion," he said. "That coward left me hanging. When we heard the door from the farmhouse open, he took off. I lay there, lying under the fence, hoping the old farmer would not see me. He must have heard the sheep squeal when we caught it. I no sooner had I slit the throat when Henk let go! I am never going with him again, he is going to get me killed! I cut up all the meat and loaded it by myself. Then he shows back up just as I get ready to leave. He helped me distribute the weight on the bike and the last two bags went on his bike. He cried like a baby, he cried like a baby. He can have what he had on his bike. I would have had to leave that anyway."

Tante Jopie came and took some of the meat. She tied it to her body under her coat.

When Pap was making plans to take and hide my uncle on a farm up north, I realized he was in the basement. Again.

CHAPTER 4

DELICIOUS HAMBURGER

The neighbor upstairs told my mother that they
would be selling hamburger around 2 P.M in the
market about 13 blocks away. She was going
for sure and my mother felt it would be good
to get what we could not ever knowing what was
ahead. We were running low on supplies but
Pap was due home soon. He was away on one of
his food gathering trips on his bicycle that
could take weeks, sometimes longer than I care
to remember.

     I always knew when Pap was gone longer
than expected: Mam would start rationing the
food and she worked harder to keep herself
occupied. We would gather greens such as
dandelion leaves on our daily walk. We would
sometimes go as far as the vegetable farmer.
We would throw stones behind the cucumbers
that were floating in the canal and then fish
them out of the water, dry them, and eat them

for dinner, sometimes with a little sugar on them. Sometimes we were lucky and ended up with two or three and Mam would put them in a jar with vinegar, but they still lasted only a few days.

Sometimes we were not so lucky. She would hold my hand while I stretched out to pick them out of the canal. I had fallen in several times but one time I pulled her with me and she was pretty upset to say the least.

Mam had a thin wooden board across the front of the baby buggy that I could sit on when I was tired, but that day I walked all the way home afraid to ask if I could ride on the board and she certainly did not offer.

When we reached the meat store, there was a long line of people already waiting. Some had been waiting since early that morning. The meat line was no different than the bread or potato line. Sooner or later someone would collapse and lay dead on the sidewalk. A horse and wagon would come, or sometimes a wagon pushed by a bicycle, and take the person away.

Mam's remark was always short and matter of fact: "I guess the meat did not come soon enough. Stand up straight - you have to be strong". I was trying very hard, but that standing in line was very tiresome.

They said there was only enough for 100 people or so. Some people left, but Mam insisted on staying. After what seemed forever, we got one pound of hamburger. We had only cheese, fruit, eggs and bread for so long that this was really a nice change of taste.

On the way home Mam planned cooking this one pound of hamburger as if it was 20 pounds. She planned some for sandwiches, some for soup and even leftovers.
It was really a feast. It tasted so good. We really did have some left over for the next day or in case Pap would get home.

When I woke up the next morning I was red under my chin. When I showed it to Mam she lifted up my shirt and discovered that the rash was all over me. The worst was under my chin. My mother got my sister ready to go out, and all that time she is yelling at me not to scratch it. "We cannot have it infected!"

The three of us left walking, and when we turned the corner I recognized the street. It was different from ours. The houses had ivy on the walls and the brick was older. We went to the door of one of the houses and a lady let us in. I think it was the doctor's wife. She greeted my mother.

My mother always paid either with two pounds of wheat or half a loaf of bread. This time she had 2 pounds of wheat. The doctor came out of the room and immediately my mother showed him the rash on my neck and chest. The doctor only looked quickly and asked if we had eaten the hamburger that had been sold yesterday, and of course we had.

He told my mother that it was at least 40% rat meat and that he had seen that same reaction already several times that morning. He told her to wash it with warm water with soda in it, or if we had no soda to use salt. If it was not gone in three days, we were to come back.

The rash went away but so did the desire to eat hamburger. That was until you got hungry again.

CHAPTER 5

OPERATION CHICKEN

The chickens meant a lot to me as a child
because they provided me with one of my
favorite foods: eggs.

The chicken coop was in the far corner of
the back yard. Even though it was primitive,
Pap was proud of the small shack-like
building. It was built from scraps of lumber
that we had found on the outskirts of the city
and along the railroad tracks. Piece
overlapped piece and the wire forming the run
extending from the coup gave the chickens an
outside area. The chicken wire was also many
pieces carefully put together and all the wire
ends were tucked in.

No one else we knew had chickens except
our milkman. Pap was always explaining to
friends who came over that we had the best egg
laying hens in the world. Four Rhode Island
Reds and four White Leghorns. A rooster was

out of the question; the neighbors already
complained about the chickens.

Every day I had to pick grass and, of
course, dig worms to feed the chickens. Since
there were only two hours of school per day,
when school was open I had plenty of time to
turn the fruit, feed the chickens and tend to
my sister if Mam had a radio to deliver. The
eight chickens laid approximately six eggs a
day of which four were traded for other foods
and corn for the chickens with nearby farmers.
Mam did not often trade in the neighborhood.
It was dangerous for people to know what we
had.

One day one of the white chickens did not
look well and it seemed to be going downhill
fast. Pap noticed a lump in its throat and
assumed something was obstructing the
passageway.

We were standing in front of the chicken
coop when Pap suggested, "If you hold the
chicken, I will just cut the skin, than cut
the little tube the food goes through and
expose whatever is stuck there. Maybe
something like a little sharp object is stuck

crossways. You don't need to look, just hold the chicken still."

He went to the corner milk store, which was empty except for milk and butter that was rationed to mothers with babies. Pap offered half a pound of wheat for two small cubes of ice. By the time he came home Mam had the cutting board ready and a pan of hot water on the potbelly stove. I held the chicken, pushing its wings against the body, pushing my hands down on the kitchen counter. I knew I better hold that chicken very still or I would be the next one scalped.

Pap took a razor blade and held it with pliers in the fire, then put it on the counter. He then put the ice cube firmly against the chicken's neck. The feathers became wet and the skin became visible. He reminded me that I did not have to look; he was numbing the skin as much as possible so the chicken would not feel the cut. He also explained the sharper the knife was the less you could feel the cut; that is why he used a razor blade.

My whole body was tense but I had to look! He made a small slit in the outer skin, to my surprise the chicken did not move. He put the blade down and spread the skin apart. I could see another layer of skin underneath. The tube had expanded so large that you could actually see the lump through the tube.

The first slit was about 1 1/2 inches long and stayed spread because of the lump. When PAP made the cut in the tube is seemed more tough and yet more elastic. Out came the ball of what looked like a rolled up watt of grass. "There it is," he said. "This is the obstruction." I was so amazed and surprised, but now what?

He instructed my mother to get a needle and black thread. Mam could not see well enough to thread the needle. Pap took over holding the chicken, which had not made a move yet. "I will hold the chicken while you sew it together, you need two hands for that." Both hands were shaking while I thread the needle. The second ice cube was applied and with shaky hands I started the job. Soon the involvement took over and I was not shaking any longer. I remember the needle going through the skin of the inner tube. The chicken did not move. The outer skin was a little tougher but I made the stitches a little bigger.

We put the chicken in a box with a hand full of corn and water. When I looked the next morning the chicken had eaten all the feed and to my surprise there was no blood anywhere. The chicken began to lay eggs again a few weeks later. I will never forget that experience.

CHAPTER 6

ORPHANAGE ESCAPE

Every time I see a freeway sign "Los Angeles"
I think of a song I learned while spending a
few weeks in an orphanage.

    "Het Angeles klept in de
verte.............
Roughly translated: The song of angels sounds
in the distance........

    Pap had gone on one of his food gathering
trips. He had decided to go southeast of
Amsterdam rather than the regular north route
because of the bombing recently in that area.

    He would stop at a farm and ask for a
place to sleep in a stall or barn and before
leaving the next morning he would exchange
food for war information. He would deliver
messages to friends and families of these
farmers - sometimes good messages, sometimes
bad.

    The Germans had taken all the radios at
the beginning of the war and, of course,

nobody had a telephone. In fact, if you got caught having or listening to a radio you were shot on the spot, no questions asked.

The S.S. officers went door to door. If there was a radio in the house, the entire family was lined up in front of the house, then all the neighbors had to come out and watch the shooting. This was a warning and example, so difficult to watch. I guess I got used to it, though. After awhile, I did not get upset any longer watching people getting shot. I just could not stand the people screaming and pleading for their lives before dying.

In fact it happened right in our own street, about the third entrance east from us. They were lined up against the wall. We were herded outside and Pap turned my face towards his leg so I did not have to look at it.

My mother never shed a tear, but her face became drawn and hard. She would not talk for hours. Pap and I went for a walk.

One day Mam got word from a total stranger that Pap had been picked up at a farm and put on a train to Germany. They needed laborers. For them to pick up a man with one arm or a woman was unusual because they were of no use to them. Mam was pretty safe since my sister was a toddler. Mam gave the man bread and thanked him for his effort, and figured Pap must have done something for him.

Life became different. Mam was short and did not talk to people. Almost every day she did take us for a walk, my sister in the baby buggy and the board for me to sit on when I got tired of walking.

Once in a while she would go alone, still taking the baby buggy. If she took the buggy without us, she had a radio to deliver and the radio looked as if the baby was in the buggy.

I did not like it when she went alone. I did not like to babysit that long!

I came home at noon from school which was just one block down the street Mam had the buggy packed, so I had to babysit. She had a radio to deliver. I knew it had something to do with my Grandmother (Pap's mother) since she had visited us the day before. During all those years she only came once or twice to visit. We usually went to her place.

Mam left with the usual instructions: "Do not go outside. Do not talk to anyone." When nightfall came and she was not home yet, I knew something was wrong.

Why did she have to deliver these radios to people; why did they listen to what they called the English channel?

I fed my sister cold cereal and one fruit. I ate an egg fried, since boiling took too long. I also had a piece of bread, and then put Else to bed.

I sat on the arm of the easy chair not far from the pot belly stove, wondering why I had to wait so long. "Should I put some coals on the stove?" I had seen Mam do it many, many times. I knew not to turn the light on -- there were no lights allowed after dark.

I carried my sleeping sister out of her crib and laid her on Mam and Pap's bed, as far to the wall as possible. I took only my shoes off and lay down next to her. It took a while to fall asleep. I don't know how long I listened intensely for someone to open the front door, but it never happened. I fell asleep.

The next morning Else woke me up. She was playing with my hair. When I realized we were still alone, I knew something had happened to

Mam. I started breathing heavily. Tears came to my eyes as I was putting my shoes on.

I put my arms up in the air as high as I could, took a deep breath, and showed Pap how tall I was even though he was not there. My face became even more serious and I was ready to start the day.

I fed us and the animals, dressed my sister, and turned the fruit in the living room 1/4 turn. It was cold in the house. The stove must have burned out sometime during the night. I did not bother with the stove. I figured Mam could take care of that when she got home.

Thank God, it was not really cold. I was stern and short with my sister who seemed to sense that she had to be good. I sang to her like Mam did and tried to fix her food the way Mam did, but I was always listening for footsteps or the front door opening.

Many days went by. I had to cut and string newspaper to use as toilet paper. We both had diarrhea from eating too much fruit.

I knew one day it was Sunday, because the church clocks rang early in the morning. Many more days went by. Our clothes were dirty, but the daily routine had become easier.

One morning I heard footsteps, then someone knocked at the door. It could not be Mam - she could come in with a key. "Mrs. van Voorst," I heard. "This is Mrs. Manderine. Is everything all right? I miss Ans in school." I recognized her voice and let her in. She was my school teacher!

She noticed right away how dirty we were and the questions did not stop. Every morning I had taken food to school for her and she was kind enough to come and check.

Later that day two ladies came. I knew somehow that we would not be allowed to stay there, so I had locked all the closets and all the doors, including the coal shed.

The keys I threw in the basement, and when we left with the two ladies I also locked the front door behind us.

My sister was crying. She was not used to other people carrying her. They took us to an orphanage not too far away. They called it a children's home.

Across the street was the park where Pap and I had seen the swans.

We got a bath and clean clothes. My clothes were way too big. That was the last time I saw my sister. Because of our age difference we were separated. She went to the baby section and I with the school children. And I was to go to school.

After a few days I learned a song that would stay with me the rest of my life. Every morning at the breakfast table we had to sing that song together.

The table was wood, we sat on long benches. Every morning a lady named Corrie would walk us to school. At noon she would pick us up in the classroom and take us back. I did not like holding her hand because it was not strong like Paps'.

I did not make friends. The ladies in charge said that I looked angry all the time. Did I ever learn to smile? And what had they ever done to me except take care of me! Many times they asked where I lived, if the house they found us in was our house. I asked if they had heard from Mam or Pap and when I asked to see my sister they answered that she was doing fine, but I never got to see her.

After what seemed a few weeks, I began to wonder who fed the chickens, turned the fruit or fed the cat. If Mam was home, why didn't she pick me up?

I hated that place! I started watching the daily routines and started making plans to get out of there. The front door was locked, and the few windows in the building were always locked too.

There was a long hallway with the front door at the end and all the doors to the different rooms came out on each side. On the other end was the staircase leading up to the bedrooms. The large dining room was on one side and the kitchen and reading room on the other. There was a bench under the stairway, next to a large door.

One day I got caught hanging around there. The lady with her hair in a bun on the back of her head screamed at me to never be there alone again. Since this the first time, and she said she liked me (I did not believe her), she let me go back to the reading room without beating me with her famous stick. I knew what the stick was and I knew where it was: in the corner in the upstairs hall way by the small bedroom. She used it regularly several times a day.

There was an old lady, who must have been in charge. She came into the reading room one day and I asked if I could see her necklace. The locket had a picture of her husband. She was not sure if he was still alive. The last she had heard was that he was in a camp in Russia.

Somehow I got permission from her to sit and read on that bench under the stairs. It reminded me of sitting on the arm of the big chair at home. I had found a substitute for my little corner I had had at home.

Several times I caught myself on that bench with tears rolling down my cheeks, but that was not allowed. I became stronger and stronger and after a few weeks in that place, which seemed an eternity, I was considered tough and mean. Nobody, not even the boys, fooled with me.

After begging my school teacher for days she went to see if my parents were back. She went several times but got tired of giving me bad news each time so she quit going.

Sitting on the bench reading I noticed that the door opened at regular times. Sometimes it was a visitor, sometimes a delivery. The visitor or the delivery man would ring the bell, announce himself, and then a buzzer would open the door automatically. Whomever pushed that buzzer must be upstairs somewhere where they could see the front door.

For weeks I watched and counted how long the milkman took, how the tall man with the gray beard took who came in the afternoon. Also, two nuns came every day, but that was always at different times.

I said I was really sick to my stomach one day. I wanted to stay home and see if my chances during school hours were better. I zeroed in on the milkman. He rang the doorbell.

When he came in he had an iron crate with 4 bottles of milk in one hand and small items in the other hand such as butter or eggs. I started holding the door open for him and he was very thankful, smiled at me and went to the kitchen.

I started counting how long he was in the kitchen and the door shut automatically.

One morning I woke up real nervous. I was leaving today. Today was the day when I would be free. I could not sing that "Angels song" one more time! I took a deep breath and put my arms above my head stretching as high as I could: "This is how tall I am, Pap," I whispered under my breath. My book was shaking. I saw the pages but could not read. I was listening for the milkman.

I saw his shadow through a small window in the front door before he rang the doorbell. I held the door open for him after the buzzer opened it and pushed the mat with my foot just far enough so the door would not latch. I took a quick look to make sure he was through the kitchen door.

I slipped out of the front door and turned left, pushing my back against the wall so whomever pushed that buzzer could not see me from upstairs. Then I slid around the corner. I did not have time to look into that candy store, so I walked on, touching the cold iron fence as I went by the church. Mam had said she would take me into that church someday. I walked home slowly pretending I belonged with the people walking down the street. Before crossing each corner I peaked to see if someone was following me, but I did not see anyone.

They must not have missed me until they were all seated for breakfast, which gave me at least 12 to 15 minutes to get home.

I could not go in the house. They would surely find me there. It would probably be the first place they would look for me. In fact I better not go through the front door, either, or the neighbors could see me. I needed another way to get in. I entered the bicycle garage several doors down the street, which had a backdoor to the back yards. I could tell the guy Mam had lost her key.

I walked all the way through the garage and never saw a soul. In fact the house looked as if it had been abandoned. The back door was unlocked and I closed it very quietly behind me. After climbing several fences I landed in our back yard.

I sat down in the chicken coop catching my breath, making sure the plans I had made for weeks were still applicable now that I was actually here.

There was one dead chicken. The big brown one started pecking at my hands. They were hungry. I picked grass from right outside the coop. I broke an egg, but it was rotten.

The next few days I ate fruit, but I remembered that I needed other foods to keep from getting sick. I could not grind the wheat because the neighbors would hear me, so I soaked it in water and then I could eat it the next day. The fruit had bad spots where it had laid too long on one side. Some was totally rotten.

I lifted the rug in the entry hall one day and lifted the shaft door, but the keys I had thrown in the basement were not there. I heard a faint meow. "My kitty, my kitty!"

I called him and called him but he did not come. I crawled to the far corner and saw him shaking, scared and very skinny. When I picked him up he went limp in my hands. I could feel his bones. He was almost dead. How could he have gotten into the basement? There was no way to get in from the outside.

The next few days I was totally occupied tending to Pimmy. I put him in a box in the chicken coop because someone would see us if we stayed in the house.

I hand fed him because he was too weak to eat by himself at first, but soon we were sharing cheese and soaked wheat. One of the chickens even began to lay one egg a day again.

Once in a while I could hear people check the door, look through the window. While rummaging through the house I accidentally found the keys that I had thrown in the basement. I found them on the windowsill in the dining room behind the drapes.

Pimmy and I moved into the house at night; it was just too cold in the chicken coop.

We made our living quarters under Mam and Pap's bed. I stayed very quiet and out of sight. The only time I was really scared was when the bombers came over. One night I woke up hearing explosions, but it sounded like a long ways away.

One evening I heard the front door squeak, that familiar squeak I had not heard in such a long time. Weeks maybe months had gone by. I listened motionless to the footsteps but they did not sound like the ones I had heard before.

The person walked through the entry hall into the living room, then into the dining room. As the figure approached the bedroom I saw it was Mam. She was scared for a moment, but when she saw it was me we sat on the edge of the bed holding each other and sobbed for a long time. We lay down on the bed exhausted and fell asleep still clinging to each other.

We were not supposed to cry. We had to be strong. But somehow that did not apply to those hours.

At daylight the next morning I could not keep my eyes off my mother. She was pale, skinny and dirty. Her feet were raw on the bottom with sores at the top and swollen. She had a huge cut on the side of her right leg. Her clothes were torn and dirty. Her beige coat had buttons missing and the dirt made it look grey rather than beige.

She told me she had walked along the railroad for what we figured later must have been close to 150 miles.

I refused to go with her to get my sister. Else was also pale and skinny when Mam brought her home.

It took months to recover. We were busy every day just surviving. I spent a lot of time on the arm of that easy chair in my own little corner, wondering when Pap would come home.

CHAPTER 7

POTATO BARGE

Pap had a friend who talked funny, walked funny, and always had a strange look on his face. I thought he should have been in an institution. He was definitely retarded.

When we would meet him on the street he would speak to Pap as if he had not seen him in a very long time, and yet he came to our house often, mostly after dark. Pap and him would sit at the dining room table and talk for hours in the dark.

He came to the house one day with a message from Pap. We had not had a visitor for weeks or maybe months. He told us Pap was in Northern Germany helping women with children cross the boarder into the northeastern Dutch province of Groningen. He would marry them and bring them across as his wife. He remembered doing this at least 52 times during the war. At least we now knew he was still alive. My mother so happy and was again real nervous for awhile, but I never expected a message that would say otherwise. Pap had told me he would be back, even if it took a long time.

A few weeks later this same man came and told my mother that Pap was in the Harbor behind the train station with a barge loaded with potatoes.

Mam walked all day, telling friends and family to go to the barge and bring bags or gunny sacks and get potatoes. Strangely enough we did not go there!

Two days later Pap came home just before dark. Even after all this time he came in the same way as always, without greeting just eye contact! He handed Mam the bicycle they took the gunny sacks off the bike and shut and locked the front door.
He looked tired. His hand was bleeding on the knuckles. He had fallen with the heavily loaded bike, but some German officer had helped him back on.

Up until today I don't remember formal greetings, I do remember sitting real close to him on the arm of the chair by the potbelly stove while he told Mam his travels and events of the past several months, whispering most of the time and without emotion.

He had been sent on a train to Germany but since he had one arm they had no use for him so they sent him on his way. Of course there are no trains going back!

He got a bicycle from a German farmer and went North, did his job for the underground organization by bringing several women across to Holland to safety.

The ONDERGROND, translated UNDERGROUND or UNDERCOVER, was an organization whose participants helped Dutch, German, French, and English people, everyone who needed help. Pap always said that there was never enough time to ask where they were from or what religion or faith they belonged to.

They sent him farther North to the Harbor. He stole a barge loaded with potatoes together with a German officer and landed at one of Holland Noethers Islands.

A farmer's wife gave the officer plain clothes and he maneuvered the barge with the current of the channel around the North Holland corner into the Zuiderzee.

After leaving the island they discovered a pregnant woman below in a corner lying on top of the potatoes. She was having her baby and could not stay silent enough during her contractions to not get noticed.

Pap did not like helping bringing that baby into the cruel, cold world. His face turned to stone remembering this otherwise blessed event.

His face looked better after shaving and my mother's vaseline treatment. It was not until days later that he confronted me with my escape from the children's home.

I was worried that he had not mentioned it sooner because he was angry and did not want to display that so soon after coming home. I was supposed to behave especially when he was gone.

Our walks were usually talk and confess times. We turned the corner and he squeezed my hand. He said he was proud of me the way I had taken care of things while he was gone. He was amazed how I had calculated my escape and best of all how I had kept from getting caught. I would make a good "Underground" worker some day he said.

He did not go on a trip for a long time.

CHAPTER 8

FIREWOOD FOR THE WINTER

Pap and I came around the corner of the Ferdinand Bol Street when we met my Aunt Jopie. She was the wife of Pap's youngest brother. She was just standing there apparently waiting for my uncle. She said they would come and visit later that day.

She looked like a prostitute, but I banned that thought out of my mind since I really liked her. To my surprise they never came to visit that day. In fact they did not show up until several weeks later.

Mam and Pap had long discussions about the coming winter. Pap needed to make one more food trip and we needed coal for the stove.

Mam and the neighbor lady upstairs went to the railroad tracks picking coal pieces and sometimes scraps of wood. It was not long until they could not walk far enough out and back during the daylight hours so with little coal gathered they abandoned the idea.

We had already cut the only tree we had
had in our small backyard. In fact, the year
before we had run out of coal in the middle of
the winter.

Pap had traded wheat for yarn, so Mam was
knitting until late in the evenings to get
sweaters ready for the winter. I wanted to
learn how to knit but she did not have the
time to teach me. I sat on the arm of the
chair watching her for hours, just talking
while she was knitting.

Every morning she woke up with red eyes,
but she kept on knitting every evening. She
got some eye drops from the doctor and at
night she put the drops in and bandaged her
eyes before going to bed.

Pap went to the South part of the city
(Amsterdam) to some close-in farmers, but the
wood he brought would only last to cook a few
meals, never mind heating the house.

Uncle Henk came over and later my aunt.
My uncle had his hand and arm wrapped in heavy
bandages up to the elbow. I don't think it was
a cast.

He asked Mam to help him change the
bandage. I don't remember why he did not go to

the doctor and I don't know who wrapped it to begin with. I had a feeling it would look bad, but somehow I had to look. His middle finger was 2/3 gone! Mam tore an old skirt of hers and my pillow case (the only one left in the house) and rewrapped that hand and put it in a sling. Pap left the room and came back with little paper envelopes with white powder in them. It must have been hidden somewhere in the bedrooms. Penicillin.
"Take this," he ordered his brother. "I lost my arm because we did not have this yet!"

The memory of that amputated finger stayed with me for a long time.

Pap told him to leave and not come back, but a few days later he came over again. That evening Pap and his brother left after dark. Mam and I went to bed.

I woke up and I heard whispering. The double windows in the living room were opened and Pap pushed a trunk of a huge tree into the living room.

I automatically began to help by very quietly taking the chairs out of the way. The whole tree went from the street through the living room, through the wooden sliding doors,

through the dining room and out the dining room windows into the backyard.
Within a few minutes after that everyone was in bed as if nothing had happened.

I laid motionless, afraid to move; listening for something to happen, I fell asleep.

The next morning I could see how big that tree really was. It reached all the way to the chicken coop.

My Aunt and uncle left with wheat, fruit and wood that next morning and came back for a second load of wood later that day. After that I did not see them for a long time.

I later heard they were put on a train to Germany where my aunt was put to work as a housekeeper for a famous German family and my uncle spent several years in a concentration camp west of Berlin.

Pap borrowed a saw with big teeth on a handle on each end. Every day I had to help push and pull until my arms were so tired I could not hold them up. Pap wanted as much as possible of the wood cut, so it would dry quicker and not lay in the rain.

He had stolen the tree a few blocks away, right in the middle of the city! The German officers on watch on the corner of the street turned their heads as he went by. They knew he worked for the underground. He told Mam often that most of those soldiers were there against their will. They also had families at home, and wished just like us that the war was over.

CHAPTER 9

THE PEPPERBUS

That crazy retarded man came over again. His
name was Heemo. He had a sister Clair who was
nuts too. Most of the times they just walked
around a block or two and visited once in a
while.

I did not know where they lived. I
wondered why they were allowed to walk around
after dark. They seemed so dumb. Did they have
parents? What did the parents look like? I
knew Heemo and Clair looked older than kids,
but they did not look like regular adults
either.

Heemo and Pap sat at the dining room
table whispering for hours one day. What did
Heemo know or what could he do? He was
definitely dumber than dumb.

The next day Pap and I went for our
regular walk. He was telling me about rumors
he had heard that our area, the south part of
the city, was going to be bombed. He said they

intended to destroy the underground electrical. 2 1/2 blocks away was what we called the Pepperbus (roughly translated 'the pepper shaker). It was a large cylinder shaped metal tank about 10-12 feet in diameter, with a pointed lid. It looked like a giant pepper shaker. Inside were large electrical meters and transformers which controlled the underground wiring. There were a few in that section of Amsterdam since that part of the city was built after 1800.

Pap said we had to get out of there, maybe to his mother's in the east of Amsterdam or all the way to Apeldoorn in the Province of Gelderland.

I wanted to ask about my kitty and the chickens. And what about all the fruit?

He had enough to worry about, not just us. We could leave, we had a place to go. But what about all the people in hiding, what about blocks and blocks of people, maybe 1/4 of the entire city?

Heemo came again and again. Pap was so busy he had no time for me.

One morning there was a huge explosion, just after dawn. I was lying in the big bed on

Pap's side. Mam was nervously making breakfast.

The windows billowed like sails in the wind and with the next explosion they blew to the outside. The pressure burst my eardrums and I screamed out with pain. Mam ran into the bedroom and she checked if I had been cut by glass. I did not have a scratch on me but my ears were hurting badly.

There were sirens, jeeps, screaming people, glass bricks and other debris all over the street. "As soon as Pap comes home we will take you to the doctor." Yes, Pap where was he? He came home minutes later. Looking straight at us he said: "The pepperbus, we blew up the pepperbus, before they could bomb it!"

They took me to the clinic, walking all the way around several blocks since we could not go past the Pepperbus. Some doctor looked into my ears and said that my eardrums were torn from the pressure of the explosion. There were no medicines left in the clinics and the doctors did not even expect any pay. The wheat Mam gave him was very welcome and he thanked her over and over.

Pap had small folded papers at home with a white powder folded in it. That was aspirin. It tasted terrible, but it made the pain go away.

I stayed in the house for weeks which had now boarded windows. Pap did not want me outside with those open ears, so he spend a lot of time telling me stories and "staying out of sight."
Diagonally across the street was a Kazerne (a German army tanker and vehicle garage) underneath the houses. The other entrance was out the other side of the block just 20 feet or so from where the Pepperbus used to be. The Kazerne is now a large Supermarket. I walked by there last in August of 1993, but I was still afraid to go in there.

My hearing loss was not noticed for several weeks. Then Pap started turning his head so I could see his face and read his lips. He spent many hours teaching me face and mouth motions and expressions. He made drawings and explained to me how the bones behind my ears would become sensitive to sound vibrations and eventually I would be able to hear.

I did not go to school until the next
September.

CHAPTER 10

PUPPIES

Since the Pepperbus explosion we could only get home by walking all the way around. Still many months later no one cleaned any of the debris. Our street was "L" shaped so going all the way around the outside of the L shade took a good 20 minutes longer.

Going through the other street we met a lady who had Chow Chow puppies. They looked like little teddy bears. Every time we went by I had to pet those little puppies.

When they were 6 weeks old I talked Pap into trading 2 pounds of wheat for a puppy. We braided a collar and leash from twine and filled a gunny sack with dried grass for a bed. We named him "Beertje" which means "Little Bear"

We walked that puppy several times a day. In fact since they had finally taken away the barricade by the Pepperbus we could go all the way around the long block.

Our food supply was getting low so Pap went on one of his food gathering trips. The second or third day passing the Kazerne entrance by myself with the puppy the giant door was slightly open and two German soldiers came out walked up to me. "What a nice puppy," they said. They picked up the puppy, pulled the leash out of my hands, and went inside the doors. I walked behind them, but one turned around and told me to go home. The giant doors shut. I went home crying. My mother walked over there with me, but the doors were shut and even after banging away on those steel doors, no one opened them.

I went back many times to see if I could see the dog, but I never saw the dog nor the soldiers again!

When Pap came home he went with me to the lady where we had traded the puppy for wheat but all the other litter mates had gone to other homes. I walked or rode my bike to school for twelve years and every time I wondered what happened to my puppy. How could anyone be so cruel to have taken that away from me?

CHAPTER 11

RAT STORIES

The canals, sewers and backyards were infested
with rats.
Sanitation was not a priority so rat
population exploded and the rats were as big
as cats, just pinkish-grey in color.

     At the Red Cross building they showed a
movie that Pap, Mam and I went to see. The
movie showed how the rats communicated with
one another as far away as one kilometer in
the sewers below the city streets. They could
stack themselves one on top of the other to
get to a piece of meat hanging from the
ceiling in the middle of a room. The movie
showed how they could slide through a small
hole and even cracks, attack livestock, dogs,
cats and humans.
They showed how a cornered rat would jump at
an adult man and bounce off ceilings and walls
to escape. They warned mothers to watch their
babies asleep in their cribs. Many had already
been attacked.

I was fascinated by that movie! We did not have many rats; at least I had not seen one for a long time.

The last one we had seen had come into the stair well from the street and crawled under the neighbor's skirt while she was scrubbing the floor on her hand and knees. She stood up and the rat dropped out from under her skirt and ran outside again. It disappeared in the gutter drain across the street.

Since the coal supply was dwindling fast Mam was only heating the house in the morning. We had dinner early afternoon, went to bed as early as 4 p. m., and read. At least Pap read out loud to Mam and me while she was knitting.

To help him study he would talk to us about examples given in his book and discuss the ones we had seen in our daily walks.

The highest floor in our apartment building was the 4th floor. Above that was a storage floor where each tenant had his enclosed storage area.

Mam would walk up 4 flights of stairs (we had no elevator) with the laundry to hang it in the storage area to dry. Often she hung it in the living room, but without heat it took too long to dry. It left the house too damp as she was heating only the living room in the mornings.

One morning she asked me to go upstairs to check if the laundry was dry. I was to bring down one long-sleeved shirt for my sister.

I liked to go upstairs because the storage area had a window and you could see a big part of the city, actually nothing but housetops and sky. It made me feel good when I could see farther than the walls of the houses which were mostly four story apartment houses.

I liked to go with Pap to the outside of the city. In fact this winter he was going to teach me how to skate. Pap had traded fruit for a pair of skates. These skates were the kind you clamp onto the soles of your shoes. I had already walked on them in the house, impatiently waiting for winter.

Pap had also spent a lot of time teaching me how to kick a soccer ball. My legs were really getting stronger. We would close the living room and dining room doors that came out into the entry hall, and the doors were then the goals. Often we would get carried away and kick the ball harder and harder when Mam would come from the kitchen to the dining room and scream that someone (she meant me) was going to get hurt.

"She is not a boy," she would yell. "Don't try to make her one!" I loved those times. And we stayed warm!

I walked up all the stairs, all eight of them. I did not have to stop to rest, like Mam, but neither did I have a basket full of laundry to carry.

I opened the door with a key. I had the keys on a thick string around my neck, one to open the front door and the second one to open the door to the individual storage area.

I had not pushed the door all the way open when a large rat scurried to the end of that narrow hallway. He crouched down against the far wall. I hesitated but entered. I did not realize I had him cornered until he positioned himself in ready to jump. I was not far from the storage door (ours was the first one on the left). and I had intentions to move closer and disturb the rat. I knew better!

Just leaning to take a step backwards was enough to scare the rat. He lunged toward me. The rat missed my throat and body and fell in front of me. I kicked that rat as hard as I could with the inside of my right foot, the way taught me how to kick the soccer ball. He hit the wall on the end of the hallway and fell to the floor.

I shut the door behind me and ran all the way down all the stairs faster than I thought I could!

Pap went upstairs with me to see for himself what had happened, and, sure enough, the rat was lying there at the end of the hallway. Pap cut the head off with the end of the shovel to make sure it was dead.

"I guess you are ready to go to the stadium with me to practice," he said. "Some of the boys will be proud of you."

The soccer team Pap belonged to practiced every Saturday. But the men leaving for the war in Germany had taken its toll. Sometimes there were only 3 or 4 men there and these were older men. I guess Pap was the youngest, and then there was Heemo, crazy Heemo, As far as I was concerned he did not count. And when

Heemo did go, he always went with us. I never
liked it when other people came with us. It
was better when it was just Pap and I, walking
and talking together.

CHAPTER 12

BURNING THE HALL OF RECORDS

As we were on one of our early evening walks,
we walked past a bakery that had been there
since Pap could remember. Once in a while we
would turn the corner just to see if the
sample birthday cake with my name on it was
still on display in the window. The display
window was bare just as the shelves inside.
There was no flour to bake very often and if
there was bread for sale you needed a
government coupon. Mothers with babies came
first, then pregnant mothers and then elderly
people, and by the time it was our turn we
stood in line at least 8 hours. People would
already be standing in line the day prior to
the sale.

     Yes, the birthday cake was still there.
It had three candles, pink roses and green
leaves. Even though I was long past the 3, I
made believe it was there just for me. Pap

said it was there since before I was born. And there was my real name right there on that cake for every one to see! Happy Birthday Annemarie.   Annemarie was my real name but nobody ever used it; my nickname was Ansje.

We walked straight to the next block. On the left was the park and on the right that terrible orphanage. Oh, I hated that place! I could not help but wonder if they still sang that song every morning.

We went to the park to see how many swans there were. There were only a few. A man walked up to Pap. They must have known each other a long time, I could tell by the conversation. After they talked for a few minutes Pap told him he would see him again sometime; he seldom invited someone to the house. I knew that was because of our food, or was it? We were lucky we had food every day; many died of starvation every day.

After silently walking towards home Pap started with: "I had not seen that guy in a long time." Pap explained to me that he worked as a statistical draftsman for the Bureau of Statistics. He drew graphs from the statistics there. That office was in a large building where all the records were kept on all the Dutch people from birth to death.

Early on in World War II the Germans were not interested in the Dutch records, but when the Germans started using their records in the large cities in Germany to capture prisoners, the Underground to which my dad belonged, considered destroying the records in Amsterdam.

Pap said they planned for months. Some people had become scared and backed out of which was already a small group to begin with. Pap remained in the group.

Early one Sunday morning in 1941 they set fire to the building. Pap said they used chemicals stolen from the Germans one can at a time; they were put in the walls of that building one can at a time. Even though only very few actually set the fire, it was a network of people who made it possible. It was not until two years later that they realized that the Jews born in Amsterdam benefited the most. At the time they burned the records their goal was to hide young men and fathers of families.

Pap was always very quiet for a few days after one of these incidents.

He would pace up and down from the dining room window to the living room window, stopping and looking out each time for a few seconds. I had my own little corner right there on the arm of that chair!

CHAPTER 13

SQUEEZED TOO HARD

Mam did not look well for several days. She
always boiled all the water we used and kept
all of us as clean as possible. Our soap was
soft and green, our toilet paper was cut
newspaper squares on a string. Pap brought the
soap from the farmers. Mam had spent many days
helping the lady upstairs when her and her
boys had dysentery and her husband was
somewhere in Germany. It is nice to help other
people, but that dysentery is so contagious
that Mam had it now. She was getting weaker by
the day. Pap went to a German doctor and paid
him dearly for white powdered medicine to stop
the diarrhea. He paid the equivalent of
$27,000 for a loaf of bread at one time. He
said the medicine for Mam was more than that.

After a few days she finally started
getting better but then my sister got sick.

We were also getting low on food and Pap
needed to make a trip. Being weak and without

food would be the end of us. Thousands and thousands had already died; at least with the medicine we had a chance. Mam began to look better and better every day. Even her frowned face brought out a smile once in a while.

She had her hands full with my sister, so Pap decided I would be better off to go with him. Where I took space on the back of the bicycle he could not put food, so he planned on only a short trip. He would just get enough food to get us over this difficult time.

Mam and Pap talked many hours before we left on that trip. They talked about my sister in case something went wrong, and Mam almost talked Pap out of taking me because I would just be a problem. But they did not want me to stay in that infested house either, so I did get to go.

Pap and I left early the next morning and by the time we reached the outskirts of the city I was already tired of sitting behind Pap on the bicycle. I had never been that far away from home. Once in a while Pap would whistle a song. Once in a while he would talk to me.

When he was quiet it was boring and I would
fall asleep.

Going with him there was a chance I would
not get sick. He himself would not get sick
because he did not have time – he had us to
take care of! That sounded reasonable to me,
and I could not change my mind now anyway – it
was too late.

We stopped at a farmhouse, he said he
knew the people, and sure enough when a lady
opened the door she was happy to see Pap. Pap
asked if we could sleep in the barn that
night, but the lady thought it would be better
if we slept in the house since I was with him.
Well, I was good for something. A dirty old
man walked in and he ate dinner with us. No
one ever said it was her husband. Pap made a
deal with them to pick up some food on the way
home within the next few days.

We slept on the kitchen floor. The toilet
was outside, and I noticed a lot of rat
droppings on the floor. We used our coats to
sleep on, but in the middle of the night it
got so cold we had to put them on. I thought
it was funny to sleep in the same clothes we
walked outside in.

The breakfast was real early. We had cereal, hot milk and honey. I had never had that cereal before. It was barley, and we had not had honey for ages.

The dirty man left early he had work to do and we left soon after that.

It would take most of the day to get to the last town, before crossing the Dike. This is the Dike that connects the provinces of North Holland and Friesland. Pap wanted to get to the farmer on the other side for wheat and then make a little loop on the way back for cheese, a whole one if possible.

I got so tired of sitting; my butt was hurting. The wind was blowing and it was cold. Pap was not cold. He was huffing and puffing just to keep us going. He even had to rest which he had not done the day before. We did not see many people. This was not like the city. This was lonesome and cold. I hid my face behind Pap's back to keep out of the wind, but my feet were cold, very cold. Pap kept saying, "We are almost there, we're almost there." It was hours later than expected when we reached another farmhouse. A real fat lady opened the door. Her husband was sitting by a large cooking stove inside; he invited us in. It was real warm inside, and it took a long time before I was comfortable. The lady kept looking at me for long periods of time. I made up my mind that I was not going to like her even though she was friendly to me.

They had heard on the radio that the Germans were going to bomb the Dike, and Pap was welcome to leave me with her while he went across to deliver certain messages and get his wheat. He could have the cheese after the messages were delivered.

This was the first time I realized that the food was not free. Pap had always said that he did odd jobs, so this was "odd jobs." I now also figured out that the reason the Germans did not want him was because he was of no use to them with just one arm. I also knew now that he not only delivered messages from Dutch to Dutch but from German to German and from German to Dutch. That is why everybody liked him!

He always said, "Everybody needs help."

We slept that night in the hayloft. Pap made a bed in the straw and covered me with

straw. It was warm and cozy. Pap looked at me
and said I was getting bigger. I know I had
been quiet and thinking a lot. "That's O.K," I
said, "but don't leave me with that fat lady
tomorrow."

It was foggy the next morning. We did
not eat nor go back into the house. We left
straight from the barn.

After a couple of miles on the bike we
stopped at another farmhouse and Pap send me
to the front door to ask for bread. Again a
lady opened the door. It was easy to ask for
bread because I was hungry. She looked me
over, then looked at Pap who was standing on
the narrow walk about 20 feet away. She gave
us bread with butter and raisins on top and a
glass bottle of milk, which Pap and I shared.

From behind the house came another dirty
old man. All these farmers were dirty and old.
This one was wearing big wooden shoes. Pap and
him talked about the English radio. I quess
some of the farmers had radios. In the city
the radios had been taken away by the Germans.

Less than an hour later we saw the
'Afstluitdijk' in the distance. The way Pap
had talked about it I thought it would be

wider. At least it was long; I could not see the other end. It was cold but not so windy. We had about 500 yards to go to the entry gate when we heard a low rumble. "Bombers," Pap said, "more than one." As the rumble got louder Pap and I got off the bike about the same time and with one move he put the bicycle out of sight in the ditch next to the road.

Pap took me by the arm and pulled me into the ditch. We scrambled up out the other side, ran approximately 40 feet, and there was another ditch wider than the first one. He told me to lie against the side like he did, not on the bottom.

We no sooner were down when we heard shooting and several large explosions.

"Lay very still. When you don't move they will probably not see you", he whispered.

Pap was very calm. That obviously was not his first time.

The planes came very low over us. Then silence, but not for long.

Pap made me move to the other side of the ditch while he stayed on one side.

This time the rumble noise came from the other side, and the noise was extremely loud.

There was dirt bouncing up from the ditch the dirt was shaking under me.

Pap threw his body on top of mine, my face hit the dirt and he was so heavy that I could not breathe. I turned my face to breathe but Pap's weight was hurting.

The noise past over and disappeared in the distance, just as it had come.

Pap rolled off of me to the side and we lay real still for a long time. It was eerie and still. Pap said he was sorry he had taken me on this trip, but he had figured the Germans would not destroy the dike since they needed and used it very often.

There were now gaping holes in the dike and we never crossed it. Our clothes were loaded with sand, our eyes and ears, everything, was sandy. We went back to the same hayloft that night. We never went to the other side.

The next morning we left with two bags hanging from the handlebars on each side of the front wheel. We had one whole cheese, butter, bacon and a few other things to eat on the trip. On the next stop, which had been the first one on the way over, we slept in the same kitchen on the floor. Pap got their corn and six bottles of liquor and coffee.

He later traded the liquor, five of the six bottles, for fruit. The fruit was carefully placed on the living room floor, and most of the coffee was traded again for potatoes and wheat.

Mam was so glad to see us and, as miracles do happen, Pap and I never became ill.

It took me weeks to digest all the happenings of that trip, but that's what my private little corner on that arm of that chair was for.

CHAPTER 14

SHAVED BALD

Most of the able men from Holland had
been shipped to Germany. There were of course
the ones that at the moment they had no use
for, like the mentally ill and the ones like
Pap who were physically handicapped. So this
left many mothers with children alone. The
younger women were every so often rounded up
like cattle and escorted to the Kazernes and
raped, often several times. Our neighbor on
the second floor, like many others, had a
German boyfriend to avoid being raped. Their
boyfriends made sure they were left alone by
their comrades.

We would see our neighbors once in a
while usually when the sirens went off and we
went to the bunkers during air raids.

I did not like to go into the bunkers.
It was difficult breathing in there with so
many people. I always got squashed. People
were always pushing. Mam would wait until the
last minute to leave the house so we would be

one of the last ones in and we would be standing close to the street opening.

There was a girl a few years older than I named Birdie. I had seen her only a few times but that was because our backyards joined for about 100 feet on the east side. The first time I ever spoke with her was after the war. She was then at least 17 or 18. Can you imagine living next door, as children, and not speaking for 7 or 8 years? I got only a glimpse of her once or twice. The parent had done a good job hiding her from the German soldiers.

Ms. Spoelder who lived on the second floor above us was not really pretty. She was always wearing a long coat and a scarf over her medium length hair. Since our bout with head lice, I was more aware of hair in those days.

Those noisy, ear piercing sirens were going again. I automatically got my coat and hat, put them on, and stood waiting by the door while my mother got herself and my sister ready. Off we went to the shelter at the end of the street. People came from all directions, a lot of women with children and older people. Then I saw the girl from upstairs running with her mother and sister. The wind blew off the hood of the one girl's head and I was shocked to see her was shaved bald. Her face was terribly bruised and swollen.

Mam talked to the mother briefly who told her that the girl's regular boyfriend had been sent south to France and the girl had refused the soldier who had come in his place.

We were in that shelter several hours which to me was a long time. I had gotten tired of standing; people were always pushing and crying.

Mam gave me a piece of cheese, but before I could put it into my mouth someone had snatched it away from me. There was no food anywhere. The people were eating the bark off the trees. There were no longer dogs and cats on the streets. We would sometimes see the body of someone lying against the wall, dead of starvation.

The "free" sirens went and we all went home again.

When I woke up the next morning Mam and Pap seemed very nervous. Pap was pacing to and from the window and Mam was working hard and getting nothing done.

They kept looking out of the windows, in the front and then in the back. What were they looking for? They had heard on the radio (the one in the crawl space under the house) that the war was ending. It was May 1st 1945. We were not going outside until Pap made sure it was safe and not just another rumor. There had been a few of those in the last couple of months.

Pap needed to also go on a food trip, but could not do so until it was safe. Beans and oatmeal were all we had left. I did not like the food, but my mother did not worry about me; my sister was the one who would never eat – she hated beans and oatmeal. Again, we were lucky that we had always some food. Most people only had what was given on coupons and that ration was down to one potato per week per person.

The only thing that bothered me was that we had no chickens left. When they stopped laying eggs, we ate them.

Pap had brought my sister and I two rabbits. When we ate them, Mam told us it was chicken but I knew better. Pap had caught them, but they were too skinny, only good for soup. Even the wild rabbits were getting scarce. The only abundance in animal life was rats. They were floating in the canals; they came right out of the toilets into the houses. People sick in bed were eaten by rats. The rats had plenty to eat because people were dying everywhere.

In the middle of the day Pap became nervous all over again. He had just heard on the radio (the station from England) that the war was over. Again Mam and Pap were looking out of the windows and pacing back and forth, back and forth. When I am thinking today I pace. I quess I did not get that from a stranger.

We were looking out of the front window. Some people had come jubilant out of their houses. Then Shots. . . . Some were dragged back into the houses.

"I told you it was a rumor, they are trying to flush everyone out to see what is left. They must need laborers." One man lay across the street for several days.

We heard on the radio that more people were shot in that single hour on that day than any other hour during the war. I guess the Germans were not giving up that easy.

On May 5th the war was finally over for real this time! We watched the German tanks leave the Kazerne. The soldiers were happy to go home too.

Pap said, "Nobody wants to be here! They are brainwashed to kill! I know many of them: that's why we are still alive."
Pap worked for and with everybody. He never asked if they were Dutch, German, English or Jew.

Canadian soldiers came with tanks, so not much changed in the Kazerne; the only difference was that there were now Canadians instead of Germans. There was still no food, drugs or clothes. The war was over but nothing changed for us anyway. In fact, the next few years were worse in many ways.

My mother became pregnant right away, and Pap got a job delivering newspapers. There were more people somehow. I don't know if they had come back from Germany or England or if they had been hiding in places like our basement.

We called it our basement, but the highest spot was only 3 1/2 feet. My uncle had cut the legs off a chair so he could sit comfortably. Most of the time he lay on his makeshift bed, looking out into the backyard through a rectangle hole behind the coal shed.

Pap heard on the radio that the Americans were going to drop food. He and I together were a good team, he said. We had very little food left, so we were ready. We slept with our clothes and shoes on to be ready at all times.

Then very early one morning I heard something different, not the sound of a bomber, that monotonous rumbling sound. This was different, all right. We ran around the corner but it was difficult to see in the distance with the tall building in the way. Around the corner we saw parachutes with squares at the bottom! Food packages!

I watched one go over our house and I figured it would land somewhere in our immediate backyards. I watched it come down slowly than faster and faster. It landed approximately two backyard over from ours. I jumped the fences keeping an eye on the parachute at all times. There were other people coming; where was Pap?

With one arm he could not get there that fast. I was there first, but within seconds others were there, but as they reached for that large box, something snapped in me! "Don't touch that!" I yelled, "It's mine. It's mine!" They still reached. I kicked and hit. I was protecting my catch very well. When I saw Pap I relaxed. "That mean kid of yours won't let us get any. This is my yard, so it is my package!"

Pap and I carried the package home. It was a huge box. We were too tired to lift it onto the table. Mam opened section by section. It contained foods I had never seen before. White flour, sugar, rice and large tin cans with very, very hard biscuits. Mam had to soak them in wet cloth to soften them before we could eat them. She started baking bread again since we now also had baking powder and yeast.

I had felt wonderful being so mean. They had called me Pap's mean daughter, and how I had acted like a wild cat, protecting that box. "You better watch that girl!" What a compliment for an eight-year-old!

The white bread with butter and sugar tasted strange. Mam was excited about the coffee she and Pap were drinking. The excitement over the coffee did not last; the next day they traded the coffee for leather – we needed shoes.

Mam cut off the tops of our shoes. She cut strips of leather and made sandals. My toes were hanging out over the front, but at least they did not hurt. She had already cut the toe section off to give my toes more room in the front, but the edge was cutting into the top of my foot. The new tops were soft. At least we had shoes – most people did not.

We had also brought the parachute home. I used two chairs to make a tent. My sister kept on breaking it down and I noticed that my mother was protecting her more and more. What I did not notice was that I was getting meaner and meaner. I walked in the street as if I owned it.

CHAPTER 15

THE SKINNY BRIDGE OVER THE AMSTEL

Mam had to deliver a radio not too far from where my grandmother, Pap's mother, lived. My sister was getting too big for the buggy. Sitting upright was uncomfortable without a backrest, but this was the only way to deliver a radio and hopefully not get caught. She did not bring the crossboard for me to sit on. The buggy was overloaded just with my sister (and the radio). With me in there too it was down on the springs and impossible to push. We walked across the skinny bridge over the Amstel River, then passed the hospital where I was born.

Mam put the radio inside a front door and walked 20 ft or so back. Someone waved a hand out the door and we continued on our way. Mam and whomever that was never exchanged a word.

Mam rang the doorbell at my grandmother's house and when the door buzzed open she carried the buggy to the first floor landing. Holding my sister by the hand I helped her up the stairs. This was one of those circular, steep and narrow stairways.

My grandmother opened the door and whispered something to my mother. We had to sit down on the floor in the hallway and wait. Mam went in. My sister was wiggling and did not want to stay seated so I hit her and of course her crying brought Mam out.

It was my turn to go in. What was up, why only one at a time?
Coming through the front door I looked directly into the kitchen. I saw three eggs on the table. I had not seen an egg for a long time.

I sat down in a chair my grandmother pointed at opposite my grandfather. He was white, not just pale, with a gray beard, gray hair and hollow eyes.

He held out his bony hand. It was shaking. He held my hand for a minute. I sat on the edge of my chair leaning forward.

"I need to see Batt," he said, then coughed. "I need to see him. You make sure when he gets home, even if it is night time, he comes to see me." With each word his face grimaced with pain. "You look just like him, and you are just like him. He was always good to his mother. He stole for her, he worked for her. If he would not have lost his arm, he would have died in the war. He got to do things for humanity that I am proud of. He has guts, he has guts......"

Those few words had made him tired. He closed his eyes. I sat there and watched him. His ears were big and were sticking out. My ears were like that and I forgot that I hated that. He had that huge dimple in his chin. Mam called it an ashtray. I had that too.

When he opened his eyes I got up slowly and promised him I would tell Pap to come and see him and I left. It was too warm in there and too stuffy. I had to get out. I knew he was very ill. I hoped Pap would get back in time.

Mam didn't let me talk a lot on the way home. She was angry with me because I had hit my sister again. Mom droned on, "You have to remember she is smaller, and that she is not strong, and that she is nicer. You should have been a boy. You are too mean," etc. etc.

I had heard the same sentence so many times, and I most likely would hear it again!

Pap came home a few days later. I told him his father was dying. Mam said that that was not what he told me to tell him, but then she admitted I was probably right.

We went that afternoon. Without telephone the only way to contact people was doing a lot of walking. Miles and miles! Remembering also how stuffy it was in their house I did not feel like going, but I had not been with Pap for a while and so I went anyway.

We went past the park, over the skinny bridge. Pap was taking big steps, his legs were so long. Finally we reached the stairs. My grandmother must have seen us coming because the door was ajar. The eggs on the kitchen table were gone. There were pears in a bowl in the center of the dining room table. Pap sat in the chair across from Opa; I slightly leaned against him. I had thought my grandfather looked bad two days ago. Boy, he looked terrible now -- sunken cheeks, his face yellowish instead of white.

"Batt, help your mother put me on the bed. I have been sitting here for days. I am tired real tired." He closed his eyes. He was breathing hard.

His bed in the far bedroom was ready. I helped make hot water bottles to preheat the bed. The room was cooler but fresher.

Oma and Pap carefully carried Opa to bed. When he lay down he closed his eyes. He was so tired.

Pap went back in the bedroom later and stayed for a long time, and when he came out, one look at Pap told me that it was all over. He died of stomach cancer.

Pap arranged to have him buried in Apeldoorn, close to where he was born.

CHAPTER 16

HOME ALONE

We did not play outside. There was still no
school so your social life and education is
what you received at home. I was lucky I had
Pap. Mam was always busy with my sister. She
also cleaned the house every day and had
deliveries to make. I had learned the alphabet
in school but Pap taught me to read.

My mother's sister Annie had a boyfriend
'Jan' whose parents gave Pap a few books for
him to read to me. When he was gone I tried
to read them on my own and got better and
better. It did not take long to go through
those few books. In fact some of the stories
I had read so often I could recite them by
heart. So I started on Pap's psychology books,
and I learned to count, to add and subtract
with money. We had stacks and stacks of money
but it was worth nothing. Some people used it
as wallpaper.

Mam had knit heavy socks and one glove for Pap. He of course only needed a left one. He was getting ready for another food trip; the last one had been a waste of time. He took the neighbor lady from upstairs, but she was pretty weak from lack of regular food and after a few miles she had gotten so tired: pedaling a bicycle takes strength. When she saw a dead body on the side of the road, half eaten by rats, she fainted. They were home two days later after stopping at only one farmer. They had only cheese and some potatoes, so Pap had to go again.

An old lady from around the corner came to ask what to do about the rats. She had one in her bedroom and was afraid it would bite her. She borrowed my cat. Nobody liked my cat because he had killed a whole nest of robins. Some ladies had seen him do it. They had been confined to their houses for months without T.V., radio, yarn or cloth, so birdwatching had become a pastime – and then they had to watch my cat kill their entertainment.

Pap and I took my cat around the corner and he caught the rat minutes after we put him in the bedroom.

After all Pap's experience and careful planning he walked into a trap. German S.S. officers came from the other end of the street and were going door to door rounding up people. First he thought someone had found out about our crawling space under the house, but at least 20 men and women were put in an army truck and then it drove away with both Mam and Pap in it.

Now what? My mind and body changed modes. That orphanage flashed through my mind. My sister was asleep - I checked to make sure she was still there.

I closed the front room drapes, then closed and locked all doors. In all the rush and confusion I had lost track of my cat. He was a big gray with yellow eyes. He was strong and healthy. I sometimes studied how he walked with the head cocked low which made his shoulders stick out. He put his paws on the ground correctly when he walked, the outside first than roll to the front toes. His body was elastic and he could make swift moves from side to side. When I tried to pick him up he would let his body go limp. I could hardly carry him he was so heavy.

That night, I carried my sister to Mam
and Pap's bed where we would always sleep if
they were not home by dark. My cat was
already there.

Several times someone had knocked at the
door during that day. I watched them through
the front bedroom window. Some I knew, some I
didn't. Crazy Heemo, Mr. van de Wedden (the
painter from across the street) and
Mrs.Mendes. I wondered if they would come
back.

I had not been to school so I did not
worry about my schoolteacher. She was the one
who got me into that orphanage the last time!
I also saw my uncle come and go, his hand
still bandaged. I was worried he would take
the food and how was I to stop him? I was just
a kid.

My sister was a problem. I hated her
crying because it would attract the neighbors.
I could never get her to that orphanage
without me getting stuck there too. When she
woke up I did not want to deal with her, but I
had no choice.

Strangely enough she was so good. I
regretted the fact that I had planned to give

her to Mrs. Mendes across the street. Mam had done that a couple of times, but I did not trust her.

In the next two weeks she hardly cried. In fact she cried only one night in bed. She might have been dreaming. I never figured she missed my mother because I was too busy and I was even too busy most of the time to think about anything.

I was so busy I forgot to watch the time and ended up doing things in the dark several times. I made sure the cat was in at night: I hated those rats.

We both slept in my mother's bed. We called it my mother's bed even though my Dad slept there too. I was a very sound sleeper and my hearing was bad, so in the morning my sister woke me up by pulling my hair. One day I happened to look in the mirror and saw that I had forgotten to comb our hair. Our hair was so matted I could not get the knots out, so I left it alone.

I had learned that to stay clean was important so I washed us every day with cold water the best I could. I only had a sink, cold water and a wash rag.

"If you cry I will hit you," was a line I used often in the beginning, but as time went by I became more sure of myself and my sister must have sensed she better be good. I cut her food in small pieces so she could eat by herself, but the cup she always used I had dropped in the sink and broken. The only thing we had to drink out of was a large milk bottle. After many spills we got better and better at it.

I cut my finger and almost fainted, and continuous earaches made me sometimes cranky. I was getting cabin fever; it would be nice to get out for a while, but that was too risky.

I took a bag of wheat, which I figured was about a pound, to the milkman around the corner, and he gave me about a liter of milk in exchange. I had been there before but never alone. I told him that my mother did not feel well and she needed some milk.

One day I took a chance when my sister was asleep in the afternoon and ran three-quarters of a mile to the farmer. He gave me a cucumber and two large winter carrots which lasted us several days. When Mam and Pap left the food supply was low. He was supposed to leave that day on a food trip, so that's why I was worried about running out of food.

I would sit on the easy chair and plan and change plans for hours. I was going to stay home and hold out until the very last of the food was gone before I would subject us to that children's home again. Besides, I really never planned on going to the orphanage; I just planned on going to Mrs.Mendes, or maybe the neighbor upstairs. I had not seen either one since Mam and Pap were gone; maybe they were gone too. You could usually hear them walk on the ceiling above us, but I had not heard anything - not any noise at all.

For nothing better to do I opened the wooden cover to the basement and I found butter, beans and juice in a large vat. I loved butter but I had only raw potatoes to put it on. The juice was good and sweet. I gave my sister a lot and I could not leave it alone either. We got dizzy and staggered and the next morning we woke up on the large coconut mat in the entry hall. I did not want to drink the juice anymore but it tasted so good. We took little sips all day long. We slept a lot those days. One day I woke up after one of my unexpected naps to find my sister with scratches all over her face and hands. She had obviously grabbed the cat and he had scratched her in an effort to get away.

My sister fell one day hitting her head on the edge of the chair. She had a pretty good lump that went away in a couple of days. She also fell in the toilet, which scared me, but I was tired of standing there and holding her. She choked on wheat kernels when I had forgotten to soak them overnight.

We were playing under the dining room table one day when someone knocked on the door, "Ans, it's me!" "Mam," I yelled. I opened the door and she grabbed my sister and hugged her and they started crying. "That rotten kid," I thought. I hated it when she cried.

Mam looked funny. Her hair was short, very short. The scars on her eyes were bigger. Her hands were full of sores and cuts.

She started almost immediately boiling water, washing our hair. We got clean clothes. We were going to the doctor the next morning to get something to heal her hands and she had not had a good night sleep in a long time. I showed her the juice I had found and promised her it would help her sleep. Of course it turned out to be a vat of cherry wine. The stains stayed in our clothes forever. I cannot remember our sweaters without those stains.

Mam and Pap had been put on a train to Switzerland. When Mam's hands broke out with large slits open sores) the family she was put to work for sent her on her way. A German soldier brought her over the border into Holland, than in a tanker to Amsterdam. At least she did not walk for days like last time. There were other people who helped others like Pap always did; maybe this was in return for what Pap had done for others.

Mam said we had changed. She said our faces were different. We grew up a lot in those weeks. She herself was different. She was silent a lot. She did not sing anymore to us before going to bed. She did not get angry at me for anything. Sometimes I wished she would so she would be the same again. My sister totally ignored me again, just as before Mam left. I was not needed any longer. I spent a lot of time on the arm of the chair.

Heemo came over, crazy Heemo, to talk to Mam. While she went to get some food for him I asked him if he had seen Pap. He said, "No."

I noticed that he was different when he was sitting in the chair than when he was standing up. This was only the third or fourth time he had been in our house. This was the first time Pap was not home. "We need your Dad's brains," he said. "He is the only one smart enough not to take chances."

He needed Pap for a job again. "Can I come sometimes?" I asked. He did not answer he just smiled. His face was different and friendly. Crazy people have feelings too. I liked him for a moment, but I realized I had a reason. "Why don't you get Pap back for me; I have been waiting too long." He said he did not know where Pap was and he was shocked when I told him that I did not believe him.

I watched him walk out the door and he walked differently than on the street. He walked straight and without a limp.
Pap came home a few days later. I don't know if Heemo had something to do with that or not.

CHAPTER 17

FOOD OR PET?

The time Mam and Pap had been gone had seemed
like months, but it had only been weeks. Pap
came back unshaven, dirty, and with a gash on
his knee, but within days after returning, he
left again on a food trip. For the second
time in a row he came back with very little.
It became more difficult to find farmers
willing to give or trade food and many farms
were run only by women whose men had been send
to camps or died in bombing raids. The tub in
our hallway had only about 6" left of wheat in
it. Some of the fruit had spoiled since it had
been only my sister and I for some time, and I
had not always tended to the fruit the way I
was supposed to.

    Mam made apple and pear sauce from the
good parts cut away of the fruit. She never
scolded me for not tending to that job
properly. The way I had taken care of my
sister must have satisfied her. I also had a

little different attitude about all the time she spent with my sister. I realized it was a whole day's job. I don't know how she got all those dirty clothes clean again, and the bed! You have never seen a dirtier bed in your life!

We heard about a farmer having chickens, but that was 4 1/2 hours walking. We did get some fertile eggs. Mam spent weeks trying to hatch those eight eggs under a lamp and warm clothes but they never hatched. That could have been my fault, too. I must have lifted that piece of blanket 101 times a day to see if the eggs had hatched.

We went often picking dandelions which Mam steamed for vegetables. But other people were doing the same thing so even those became harder to find, and we had to walk farther and farther. By now people were cooking grass and tree bark just to stay alive.

Somehow we ended up with two rabbits. I immediately assigned one to my sister and one to me. Mam left them outside in the chicken coop, even though I asked her 1000 times if they could come in the house so we could play with them. That never happened. There was a white one and a gray one. I liked the gray one the best. The white one was timid and reserved, probably younger. The gray one was feisty and aggressive. I figured my sister would end up with the white one anyway. She always had first choice and Mam always reminded me that she was so much smaller than I was.

I went to the chicken coop several times a day and fed that gray one some grass and green leaves that I stole from the jasmine tree next door. I could touch his nose and study his face. Every time he would hear the slightest noise he would stop chewing and his nose quit wiggling. His nose always moved first before he started chewing again. Maybe he reminded himself of what he was eating. I avoided touching his whiskers because than he would pull back. I did not want him to be afraid of me.

The fur was soft and smooth; touching it gave me a good feeling. If I touched him too hard and felt his body and bones he would jump away. I promised him that if he would let me touch him I would not hurt him.

One evening when Pap sat on the side of my bed to tell me a bedtime story, he had to clear his throat. He started, "We have been eating a lot of the same foods lately and we need something more substantial. The hamburger we ate was from a cow and in nature animals kill animals to survive. Time has come for us to eat the rabbits." The gray one was the biggest and fattest, the white one needed more time to fatten up! I knew why that gray one was the fattest and the biggest. How could we eat it?

Pap went on to explain that he would knock it out with one hit on the back of the head and then kill it so it would never feel the pain. I only heard part of the instructions because all I could think of was that it was my fault he had gotten so big and fat. The worst of all I had promised him I would never hurt him! I had fed him secretly every day, and he let me touch him. It took a long time before I fell asleep. I wanted to cry but I became angry instead. I was so mixed up and the morning came all too soon.

When Pap saw that I was avoiding him and too quiet he decided to get it over with as soon as possible. With one hand Pap opened the cage and I picked up the rabbit carefully. I held it real close to me and could feel his heart beat against my chest. While I walked in front of Pap from the chicken coop to the kitchen I whispered to him over and over, "I am sorry, I am sorry. I did not know." The rabbit put his head under my chin and sat so quietly in my arms. He was not afraid.

Tears ran down my face when I put him on the kitchen counter, but I was not crying. I became stone cold. As per instruction I held its feet between my fingers, the front feet in my left hand and the rear feet in my right hand.

Pap hit him with the side of the hammer behind the ears. He fell limp on the counter. He never put up a fight. I held the limp head back and Pap slit the throat, then cut the skin all the way down the chest and stomach and peeled it off.

I never ate a bite, not even the soup. God knows it smelled so good and I was so hungry! The bread and cheese I had come to hate tasted wonderful.

I sat on the arm of the chair often those days, thinking a lesson I had learned (at least that's what Mam said). I don't know what lesson it was or even if it was a lesson at all! I had learned to guard my feelings before, but after this affair I became hard and sometimes bitter.   Months later, maybe as much as 10 months later, I finally found a way to accept this by making myself believe it was not Pap's fault. He did not know, because I simply failed to tell him, that I not only had made a special promise to this animal, but the reason he was big and fat is because I fed him extra every day.

I also came to terms with myself that I had no business putting feelings into an animal that was food and not meant to be a pet. Boy, I was pretty stupid!

Even if all this reasoning was self preservation, it worked and my broken heart healed within time.

CHAPTER 18

CHAIN LINKS

On Pap's second trip he came back with rice
and jam. I had never seen rice and jam before.
I loved bread with butter and jam and the rice
was a change from that wheat and oatmeal that
had been our major food for at least 5 years
now. Pap had picked this up from a German
outpost outside of Amsterdam.

      On one of our walks to the park we met
Heemo. Pap did not acknowledge him but kept on
walking. Heemo walked behind us a few feet.
Heemo talked and Pap listened. He had heard
that there would be a raid on the homes in the
East of Amsterdam, which was 80% Jewish. He
wanted to know how they could warn the people.
It had to be done that day.

      Instead of going to the park we walked
past it on the opposite side of the street. On
the end of that long block we made a right and
at the next corner a left again. Half way down

the block Pap told me to sit on the step and not move until he came back. He went up the stairs and came back in just a very few minutes. A lady came down behind Pap and started walking. We followed approximately 100 ft behind her.

I knew better than to ask where we were going! We followed that lady for many blocks. We had made so many turns I was totally lost. Until almost dark we followed that same routine. I sat on the step. Pap went to visit someone and when he came out a few minutes later another lady would come out and we would follow her for a while and then do the same thing again.

In this routine (called chain link) everyone was warning everyone block by block of what was about to happen. We got home just before curfew, which was at dark.

The next morning Pap was already gone when I woke up. I did not bother asking where he was because I knew the answer: "He had things to tend to, he'll be back shortly." "Shortly" had been 30 minutes, but "shortly" had also been as long as eight months.

Mam rushed us to get ready. We went with the baby buggy to the same neighborhood Pap and I had been the day before. It looked different now. All the doors were open, all the windows broken, and furniture, lamps and other belongings spread all over the streets. We walked a few blocks through the rubble and went home.

Pap was already home. He told Mam that most of the people got out O.K but there was not much left of their belongings.

CHAPTER 19

YOU BETTER LOOK . . .

Again unrest was building. This time
something had happened with England. Pap kept
track of things by going into the chicken coop
to listen to the radio. It was turned so low
that he had to have his ear pressed against it
to hear it.

There was also again trouble in the
Heineken Brewery. The men who were put to work
there were hungry and weak so beer production
for the troops did not go smoothly.

Pap and I walked towards downtown and
then turned right along one of the canals to
visit Mrs. van Dam. This is two houses down
from where Anne Frank's story took place. That
lady was so happy to see me. She kept looking
at me and touching my hair. I had seen her
before, but I could not remember if it was in
that same house or that she came to visit us.
She asked Pap several times if Mam was O.K.,
and when we said goodbye she had tears in her

eyes. I thought she should have waited with her emotions. I reminded myself that that was not the thing to do. She should have waited until we were gone; at least that is what strong people like us did.

When we came to the corner Pap decided to not go downtown but to go home. After a few blocks of walking we saw a large group of people ahead. There was a traffic circle just before the bridge over the Amstel, and across the bridge was the brewery where the Weteringschans crosses the Ferdinand Boll Street.

On the grass area by the bridge were, I think, seven men lined up. The Germans were gathering everyone in sight to watch their "demonstration." They were all brewery workers, people who lived close by and people who were passing by like us.

The soldiers shouted to the audience that these men had not followed their rules and/or instructions. Everyone there was to look so they could learn a lesson and if you looked away you would join the line up.

It was so quiet, so still, you could hear everyone breathing. Pap told me to hold onto his leg and to not let go, regardless of what happened.

The first shot was loud it made my whole body shake. People moaned, some fell to the ground. Pap had put his hand in front of my face so I could not see the men fall.

Again they yelled the same warning, "If you look away you will be next!" The second shot was louder than the first. It made me wet my pants. I was cold, very cold. I did see body parts fly all over, but I had seen that before. It was the sound that bothered me.

To keep their promise they took one person out of the crowd, I think it was a lady, and shot her next. She cried and pleaded but it was over quickly.

Then the next and the next and the next........I held onto Pap's leg as tight as I could. Finally Pap squatted, picked me up mumbling while he walked away, "Why did they have to blow them apart?" It had been a long time since he had carried me. I thought I was too big for that now, but I was glad I was wrong.

The next few days were strange. Mam and Pap argued over me going with him all the time. They never argued. Mam wanted to avoid the trauma that came always unexpectedly.

I did not like it that I had been the cause of their argument, but it did keep me on the arm of that chair thinking about it and hoping that I could still go with Pap.

Maybe Mam did not know that we were a team. After all I did not cry. I had only wet my pants, but that was because of the noise!

I have seen the memorial stone there from a distance when I went by on the tram, but I have never stopped. I will never stop. Now more than 50 years later I can still hear those blasts. The soldiers wanted to make an impression on all the people there. If everyone who was standing there remembers it as I do, they sure did a good job.

CHAPTER 20

TONSILS

The weather change brought problems. Winter was cold, but the bacteria stayed low or less effective. As soon as it became warmer diseases spread faster.

So I came down with chicken pox. Since our doctor, like most Dutch doctors, were in Germany or with the troops in France, Pap had to find other sources. After a ten-day search he had found one, A German doctor in one of the smaller hospitals, Klimophuis, translated Ivy House.

Pap took me over there and I sat on a chair in a small room. We talked about counting my spots, and that if they were black instead of red I would have been a Dalmatian. Then Pap had always a story to go with it. Most of the main characters in his stories were happy-go-lucky, yet sly and smart. Pap was teaching survival in some way or form every day.

Since I had had a bout with 'ratburger' the doctor assured Pap that it was definitely chicken pox. "Do nothing. Keep clean." Pap paid him with money. I had not seen him do that in a long time. Maybe the German doctor thought it would be worth a lot once the war was over.

After a couple of weeks I was back to normal except my ears were hurting a lot. I did not complain about my ears because of the results of the chicken pox I had given to my sister. My sister Else became very ill and of course I had given the chicken pox to her. I felt bad, because Mam had so much extra work, but I don't really know how that got to be my fault. I did not go anywhere with Pap for a while.

Mam spent every minute of the day tending to my sister who had become very bad. She had a high fever and her body was swollen from head to toe. The same doctor I went to gave Pap some white powder wrapped in square pieces of paper for my sister, but by the time her fever finally broke my mother was exhausted.

I sat hours on the arm of the chair reading Pap's books, holding my ears. By now the slightest noise would cause sharp pains.

Pap took me back to that doctor. He was younger or close to the same age as Pap, round friendly face, but I also noticed his big hands. After a quick look he motioned Pap to come outside the room. I knew something was wrong because I could not hear people talk when they were not looking directly at me. I don't think that doctor even realized how well I had learned to lipread. My hearing was supposed to have become better after that blast from that Pepperbus, not worse. "Pockets" as he called them just past where my eardrums were supposed to be. My tonsils were so large that I could hardly swallow.

A large chair in a room at the end of the hall looked like a dentist chair. He strapped me in there and I can only remember pain. If I would sit real still he would lance some of the abscesses. He did not waste any time. Blood and pus ran out of both ears. He gave Pap instructions and a date to come back.

I had to wear a cap, which covered both ears and a scarf over that. Cold air nearly killed me so I was happy to oblige.

Mam looked tired and weak. Her eyes became progressively worse. That last trip to Switzerland, my sister sick for two months, lack of proper food, and of course all the stress, began to take its toll on her health and nerves.

As a child of eight years old her eyes had been damaged by a childhood disease and the scars were blocking her cornea. So as the scars became bigger her vision became worse.

My second appointment with that doctor was to get my tonsils peeled. I went the night before and they put me in a baby crib because it was the only bed available. Lying down I could touch the top of the rails easily.

Early in the morning they put me in that dentist chair again. I saw Pap standing just outside the door. He put up his thumb: "Hang in there kid, I am right here." Then they put a cup over my face and I dreamed about the milkman throwing milk at me.

When I woke up I was in that crib. I hated being in there. It was like being in jail, like that orphanage. Pap stayed with me. He left only long enough to go to the bathroom.

The second or third morning he said he was leaving to get food. We all needed to get our strength back after all that had happened. A few days later a lady came and helped me get dressed. Outside was a horse and buggy to take me home. Pap somehow had always something special!

Mam was waiting for me at the front door and put me in her bed. I was so glad to be home! I could eat only soft for a while and my ears needed cleaning 3 times per day. Eating soft meant oatmeal. I hated oatmeal!

Pap came home that afternoon with his bicycle loaded. Mam helped him get it up the steps into our entry hall and locked the door, all without speaking.

Pap had brought a lot of butter. Even oatmeal became edible with a spoon of butter in it. And potatoes and butter. Boy did I eat!

It took a long time for me to get really well, as I remember it took several months. Pap said that German doctor got paid well, and when Pap said he got paid well that meant a lot! I had to keep cotton in my ears all the time and that scar tissue would form and eventually function as eardrums.

The bones behind my ears needed to become sensitive to sound vibration. Every day Pap and I would practice. My ears were stuffed with cotton, then I covered them with my hands and Pap would say words standing behind me. First he was standing real close, then farther and farther away. I was allowed to turn my head slightly and I still do that today.

We heard that the schools would reopen for short parts of the day, maybe even 5 days per week. I had not been reading a lot lately and Mam suggested Pap better find me something more appropriate to read than his psychology books. Sure enough, Pap came home with a big storybook of Hans Christian Andersen.

On the days Pap was home I had my own continuing soap opera. The main character was "Elf Bighead." Even my sister was beginning to listen to some of the episodes.

During the summer my sister came down with German measles. At least that is what we call it now. In those days it was just called measles. Just like with everything else she got, she became very ill. I was glad I was not the first one to get it this time. No one could blame me for this one!

Pap had 2 different doctors come to the house. Both suggested to keep her room dark until her eyes were better. It took six weeks before her eyes looked better. Her body had healed in a lot shorter time.

I spent time reading those Andersen stories over and over; Pap went on another food trip; and Mam spent days and nights tending to my sister worrying that her eyes would be affected as hers were years before.

There was an apple tree three yards over, and I went to steal the fruit two at a time. I never got to eat much of them myself since my sister needed to get well. Maybe that is how that got started, because since then if there was a small amount of something it had to be for my sister.

She was a beautiful child, gorgeous hair, but frail and always sick. She ate so little, so whatever she wanted she could have.

The first trip Mam made with us in what seemed forever was to see her father. He was in charge of a factory that made sugerbeets into sugar, syrup and candy. As we walked into the big open warehouse he came out of the cellar. He was short, his legs terribly bowed and his face weathered. He looked at me and smiled, looked at my sister and commented that she looked like their family. Mam and her father did not hug or even shake hands.

She handed him a large green can and he left to the back of the building. He brought it back filled with syrup and Mam put it in the corner of the baby buggy so it would not tip over.

It was a short cold visit, but at least we had syrup for pancakes. In fact we had never had that before.

The building was cold and drafty. It was also almost empty except for a few large vats. Maybe there was more down those steps but we never looked. Mam said goodbye again with no hug or even a handshake. This was not the first time I saw my grandfather. There was one time prior to that and twice after.

CHAPTER 21

A GERMAN SHEPHERD NAMED ROBBIE

Mam got a message from a strange lady one day
that her father wanted to see her. She had had
contact with some of her brothers and sisters
but not often. Her sister Annie lived with us
for a while before the war started and she was
the only one I knew well.
Tante Annie was hiding with her husband
somewhere in the North of Holland. If
something was wrong with her, the message
would not have come via Opa Happe's house.

   Mam did not feel like going. She was
walking nervously around the house. No sooner
had she decided to go than she would change
her mind again.

   I knew better than to ask questions, but
why would you not want to see your father? I
was always happy when Pap came home!
My grandmother had died (Mam's mother) when my
mother was only 16 years old. She left the
house shortly after that. My grandfather

remarried to another lady whom I was to call "Tante Too"(Tony).

We did leave the next morning and walked and walked and walked. I did not think we would ever get there. When we reached the main train station I thought we were almost there, at least that is what she had said the day before!

We went across the harbor called Het IJ on the ferryboat. I loved that ride: the wind in my face and so much water! When we reached the other side I decided to ask Pap to take me there more often and go back and forth on that boat all day long. Now I could hardly wait to visit because then we could go back on the ferryboat again. Mam said again that we were almost there.

She showed me how they had built houses and put streets and trees on top of the Fokker Airplane factory to hide it. This way the bombers could not see where the factory was. They looked like real houses at first but then you could see they were empty and some only had two sides.

We walked through a tunnel, which I thought was an elongated bomb shelter. It

smelled bad in there. There was urine and
vomit in the corners and on the walls and Mam
had a difficult time maneuvering the baby
buggy around all the bad places. She warned me
not to touch the walls or step in shit; she
yelled so loud it echoed!

When we came out the other side she
rolled the buggy back and forth in the grass
to get the wheels clean and made me wipe my
shoes on the grass. It was good to smell fresh
air.

Just a few blocks farther Mam walked up
some steps and rang the doorbell. A lady
opened the door and just stood there looking
at us for what seemed to me a very long time
when a man's voice invited us in. We were in
the kitchen. There was a table and four chairs
in the middle of the kitchen, a wooden chair
with arms on the right, next to that a large
pillow on the floor, and next to that the
stove.

Mam motioned me to sit on one of the
chairs and she sat on another holding my
sister on her lap. Opa sat on the wooden arm
chair. I heard other people in the house
talking but I could not see them. On my left

was another door opening through which I could see another room, which I thought could have been the livingroom; it seemed a little dark in there.

My grandfather called, "Robbie, here!" Out of that room came a large German Shepherd dog into the kitchen. Opa said"Af!" which meant "down" and the dog laid down on that large pillow between Opa's chair and the stove.

I could not keep my eyes off that dog. I had never seen anything like it in my life! His eyes were bright, his nose black, his ears straight up. I knew he was smart. If I could only touch him! I leaned forward. "He is not a bad dog," Opa said. "Just leave him alone. I take him to work with me, so he can watch the goods. No one steals when he is with me. He does not like children – they make him nervous."

I figured Opa had read my mind, but I still had to look.
Every time I looked away or wanted to listen to the conversation, I found myself looking at that dog again. I knew the dog was not afraid or nervous. If I could pet him I would be

gentle and make him feel relaxed, I would bet anything him and I would get along regardless of what Opa said. I wondered what would happen if someone tried to run away from him, or hurt my grandfather. I could see the big fang teeth when he panted. I bet they could do a job on someone's leg or butt.

Then I heard Mam say that we were leaving, we had a long way to go back. I had to say goodbye to Tante Too! She was not my Aunt, why should I call her Aunt? She was a stranger. She looked my mother's age. She had a phony laugh. In fact for weeks I imitated her.

Because of the dog that drew my full attention, I never heard why we had gone over there. The ferryboat was cold on the way back. The wind had come up and it was later in the day. I pretended the dog was walking with me all the way home. We were exhausted and glad to be home. This would not be the last encounter with the German Shepherd world.

CHAPTER 22

DUMB BOYS!

All that money that I had learned to count
with was worthless! New money was issued and
it was O.K,. I quess, but my mother complained
there was still nothing to buy. Pap kept on
making his regular food trips and we grew some
stuff in the back yard that I did not like.
One of the few things we bought were tokens
for the electric meter, so you bought your
electricity in advance.

People kept reappearing, some with horror
stories from Germany and Russia, and some had
been hiding in England. We had now a little
radio hanging above the sliding doors between
the living and dining rooms, so we could hear
it from both rooms.

Pap kept listening to the news every
evening at 6 P.M. when he was home, but all
this freedom and promises made our lives worse
rather than better.

We still did not have the lights on after
dark, this time not because of "blackout" or
"curfew," but because we had no money to buy
the electric tokens to put in the meter. We

had less food. The farmers had run out too. Women and small children were working the farms to build production back up.

Most men never returned, but the ones who did were wounded, ill or so undernourished that it would take years before they could do heavy farm work.

The Kazerne (the German army garage) was still a garage, only now it was occupied with Canadian soldiers. They were friendly, gave us gum, but we were not used to people being friendly. I used to stand and watch them. My feelings were sometimes so mixed up. I had been taught what to do with the German soldiers, and if I disobeyed the results were bad. So to watch these men without instruction was a new experience, with new feelings and mixed up thoughts.

Mam and Pap had talked about more and better food, maybe toys. The only toy I owned was a rag cloth doll Mam had made for me. But I had outgrown that long ago. I just made sure my sister did not touch it!

One day, while standing by our front door, I watched some of the neighborhood children hop on a tanker to go for a ride.

Most of them were older than I and I did not even know all of their names. It was only recently that school had started on a regular basis and I kept my distance.

I did well in school. Pap had taught me enough to pass 6th grade, but I had developed that mean and bully image. One of my lines was, "Don't be nice to me, so I don't have to be nice to you!" So my teacher, bless her heart for trying, suggested I go to story-time hour on Wednesday afternoon. I had skipped from 2nd to 4th grade, and the boy who was supposed to take me was a 4th grader. He had red hair, freckles and had actually become my "boyfriend" for a short time. It was about a 45-minute walk so there was a lot of time to talk. We found we had something in common!

He told me his mother and dad wanted another child but they wanted a girl this time and he had no idea how they were going to go about that. Mam and Pap had discussed at length that they wanted a boy now that the war was over and the odds were in their favor since history showed that after a war a lot of boys were born. In fact 7-1 were the chances of getting a boy. I knew all this; I had read a lot of Pap's books.

The first Wednesday we never got to our destination. Henry and I got into a heated debate about this very important brother and sister issue. I could not figure out how he could possibly want a sister. I offered for him to live with mine and I assured him he would then change his mind.

Then I realized he did not know that parents had to have intercourse to have babies. I explained to him that his father would lay on top of his mother and that his penis would go inside her. His eyes just about popped out of his head. He said that his parents would never do a crazy thing like that!

I tried to tell him about my cat and other animals that lived, but he made up his mind that his parents would never do that, no matter what! "How do you think you got here, dummy?" I left him standing and went home.

When we got to school the next day the teacher (a very good friend of Pap) wanted to know why we did not show up at that "Story-tell hour" the previous afternoon. Henry told

her it was my fault, that I had said that his
mother and father were crazy and dirty. They
did not do things like I said they did. I was
upset that he blamed everything on me, not
that he was stupid and did not understand.

The rest of the school day I brewed over
that and when school was finally out I waited
for him outside. I stood sraight in front of
him and asked him to explain to me why he
twisted the story so badly, so it had become
totally my fault. I lunged at him and beat and
hit him as hard as I could. When I had him on
the ground I put my foot on his throat and
made him promise to never ever do that again.

The next morning his mother came to
school with him. "What a chicken," I thought.
Then out of spite I mumbled to myself, "Even
though you are a nice looking lady, you have
to submit to your husband if you want another
stupid kid like him!" Henry's face was black
and blue and he had scratches everywhere on
his arms and face. Mrs.Godron (Margareta
Godron), my teacher, told me to go get my dad
and meet her in her office.

I walked the one block home slowly and on
the way back to school I told Pap what I had

done. He did not say much but when he took a look at Henry he turned abrupt and gave me a puzzling long look, but not a word was said. They asked again what happened and Henry stuck to his story like glue. He could not accept facts (my facts) even after that beating I gave him.

On the way home (I was sent home for three days) Pap explained to me that the world in school was different than at home. He was proud of me that I stood up for myself and he said that Henry had a lot to learn. Maybe Henry did not have cats and dogs, maybe Henry's Mam did not tell him about the birds and the bees.

The teacher took me herself to that next story-time thing, but when I discovered they were Bible stories I never went back. The lady telling the stories was too sweet and the feeling in that room was wierd. I had never heard about God before, and whatever they were talking about my life did not seem to fit in there. I did see why Henry should go every week, but I had no use for that!

Besides I was right again! My mother had a boy in March of 1946!

CHAPTER 23

TEACHER'S PET?

My sister and I had only first and last names,
no middle name. The girls in those days were
not as important, or maybe it was just a
custom. My brother had a first, middle, and
last name. I don't know where 'Robert' came
from, but his middle name Lambertus is Pap's.

In fact my sister's and my names are very
short: ANS and ELS, three letters each. I had
counted my brother's: 15 letters! the most I
had ever seen in a name. Mam had told me she
was going to have another baby and it was not
long after that that her belly began to show
it. It was not until then that the fact became
real for me.

I asked her often how she knew it would
be a boy. I could not imagine another sister.
That thought slowly became a nightmare. Even
worse, I had to start taking my sister
everywhere I went: to the baker, to the
milkman! She walked so slowly and talked too

much. Stupid stuff! She picked up rocks and stopped a lot. Strangers would stop and look at her. She was cute and friendly: frail, with rosy cheeks and blond curly hair. They called her "Sunshine".

Our school had a lot of kids. After being called Froebel School, it was now called the 9th Montessori School. My teacher, Magareta Godron, became the principal of the school but remained also a teacher in our classroom.

We had been told weeks in advance that a lady named Maria Montessori from Italy would come to visit. Mrs.Godron was so excited and she told us just about every day something about Maria Montessori. The teaching method used in our school was based on the child psychology of Froebel, but the didactic materials used were invented by Maria Montessori.

Froebel stressed to use as many senses as possible and the materials made it a hands-on lasting impression. There were sandpaper letters to learn how to write the letters by touching them in writing motion. There were color tablets to match colors and learn shades. Insets taught small muscle coordination and dexterity. Cylinder blocks were used to teach perception. We counted rods to learn numbers up to ten, etc.

She had designed these tools in Italy and perfected them using them on Rome's poorest and most deprived children. She even had retarded students. She wrote many books for parents and teachers explaining and showing why Froebel's method and her materials worked so well together. Mortemar Standing also wrote books on the Montessori method. A well-known one is Montessori Mother.

Finally the big day arrived. Pap, now on the school board, of course came with me that morning. Mam always put bows in my hair but that day I even had an extra bath. Our normal bath was on Friday, but to get a bath in the middle of the week was only on special occasions.

Pap and I always formed an opinion about people, the way they walked, talked, acted etc. So after hearing so many stories about Maria Montessori I had a definite opinion about her. I figured she would be friendly since she worked with children and she must dress well in bright colors (people liked that

on my sister) and I guessed she must be tall
to be smart and she must be wearing
glasses if she read a lot. In fact, if she
was as smart as my teacher said she was, her
eyes were probably worn out like my mother's.

Our classroom had a podium on the wall,
and behind that was a blackboard. On the left
side were windows and on the right side
shelves with Montessori materials. Pap had
brought paper and new pencils.

Even our materials were polished. Our
tables and chairs were clean and the wooden
floor free of dirt. There were still marks
where our shoes had made grooves and dents
from the chair legs, but most of the paint was
gone from the table tops and the chair seats.
(We had individual tables and chairs). The
mats we used to work on on the floor were
clean. The geraniums in the window sills
looked crisp. All the dead leaves were gone
and the pots and saucers were clean.

Mrs. Godron really liked me even though I
did not talk a lot. At least she thought I
was smart. In fact she was one of the few
people who had seldom said anything bad about
me. She did not complain that I looked stern

all the time. She never seemed to notice that
I picked my nose, (which I did); she never
pretended to like the bows in my hair. I did
not like the bows, especially when people
noticed. Those bows were certainly not my idea
- it was Mam's idea of looking good.

Even after that big fight with Henry,
when I returned to school, she never mentioned
it again. Some parents were still talking
about it months later. They called me mean,
stubborn, tom-boy etc., but Mrs. Godron seemed
to have forgotten about it.

I used to watch her when she was working
with other children. As I am thinking of that,
she was a little stern too! I wondered if she
was married; maybe she had a sister like mine!
She walked secure as if she knew where she was
going. When she was called out of the
classroom she walked hard, her feet in rhythm
hitting that wooden floor. She was tall. She
had a gray skirt. I never admitted that I
liked her. Once you are taught as a child to
not trust or like anyone, those feelings don't
go away just because they say the war is over.

The classroom door opened and Mrs.
Godron, Pap and a lady dressed in black walked

in. She was wearing a black hat, black dress, black shoes, black overcoat. Her face was dark. I figured she had been outdoors a lot.

"This is Madam Maria Montessori," said my teacher. I did not hear the rest as I was watching that lady. I wondered if someone had died in her family, maybe her husband? She looked poor and sad, and all black was not my color. That was not at all what I had expected. Her shoes looked like black army shoes with heels, although she did not hit the floor like Ms.Godron. Maybe those psychology books of Pap were all wrong, except for her small head which was supposed to mean she was smart. But that hat had to go!

I heard my name, at least I thought it was..."She is already doing 5th and 6th grade work." Then Mrs.Godron asked me to come up to the podium. I walked slowly even though Pap had said I had to walk as if I was sure of myself.

I looked at the door, but Pap had left. I did step onto the podium in the middle, which was a big step rather than the extra step at the end by Mrs.Godron's desk. I stood next to Maria Montessori who now had her arm around my waist. She had a firm hold on me and smiled. It was so quiet in the classroom. She petted her leg motioning me to sit on her lap. I did not want to do that!

Mrs Godron came to my rescue just as I sat down on her lap. She explained to her that I could not hear her unless I was looking directly at her, so she allowed me to stand up again.

She told me I was a real Montessori child, progressing at my own speed and helping other children along. "We can let her skip a grade, she is mature enough. I already spoke to her father".

Well, that seemed nice enough, but I still did not like her black clothes and that hat. I wished Mam could see that one! I read in Pap's books that some people wear a hat to cover up their hairline or wrinkles.

Pap was busy while Maria Montessori was in Amsterdam. Days later Pap and I had a chance to talk about her. Pap was amazed at her perception and knowledge about children, how she wanted to educate more parents and teachers. She made teachers start in Kindergarten and work their way up to the 6th

grade, so when they taught the upper grades
they knew the total background and development
of the child.

        I did not tell Pap that I did not like
her clothes, her hat..... I never mentioned
that she did not impress me at all.
We did talk about high and low foreheads and
that red hair usually indicated musical
ability. I did not remember that she had any
hair, except that black bun on the back of her
head. I was the first child to ever skip a
grade at that time in the Montessori system.

CHAPTER 24

ROBERT

Mam began to look very pregnant. Her eyes
were always terribly red and she blamed it on
the knitting she had done. I knew that baby
had to be a girl again; otherwise she would
probably be doing better. Whatever went wrong
I could figure out a reasonable way to blame
it on my sister. It never entered my mind
that I was a girl too. I had an explanation
for that too. I did not cause all the trouble
my sister did.

Visitors always liked her! The nickname
"Sunshine" had become well known. Of course I
did not have any special names, but that was
because I did my own thing. I had 2 old socks
full of marbles. Mam would always make me give
some to Else, but she would just lose them
again to other kids. I either had to beat them
up or win them back, because Else would go
home crying and then I was in trouble anyway.
It was a no-win situation.

Then there came the time when the kids would not play with her any longer so I let her roll mine once in a while. We started playing ball in school, one a game with 2 tennis balls, a sort of juggling against a wall to the rhythm of a song. My mother had done that when she was a child so with her help I learned quickly.

The tennis balls took the place of the marbles, and my sister lost those just the same.

In the street where we lived the kids we played with knew well enough to leave her alone and not steal from her or cheat, but when she started school it became more difficult to keep track of her.

Robert Lambertus van Voorst was born on my mother's sisters birthday, March 25th. There were so many children born in those 10-12 months after the war ended. My brother was born in the hallway of the hospital on a cot. An old army cot. Not enough hospitals, not enough beds, not enough doctors, not enough nurses.

I was overjoyed when Pap came home with the news that the baby was a boy. I felt that

that was done just for me! After all the trouble with my sister, I deserved something better.

I went to see Mam on the 3rd or 4th day. The baby looked just like me, she said, though both her eyes were bandaged. The doctors said she needed rest and her eyes covered so they could heal.

Pap and his friend Harry moved the whole house around before Mam came home. My sister and I went into the dining room, beds and all. Our beds folded against the wall, so every night the beds were folded down and in the morning folded up again, closed off with curtains.

We were each on opposite sides of the room with the dining table and chairs between us. Our own shelf above the bed was the first space I had that really belonged to me. That became a cozy corner and I did not sit on the arm of that chair any more.

Mam and Pap's bed went in our bedroom and a lady named Corrie moved into Mam and Pap's room. That door had to stay shut and we were not allowed in there, not even by invitation! In exchange for rent and food this lady helped

Mam with the baby and took care of my sister. She even cooked some meals. I finally found some long lost freedom.

On Sunday morning some friends of the family came to visit and Mam told me to take my sister for a walk. If I hurried and took the short cut I would be able to pick some flowers for Mam in the park.

We made good time on the way over and I had a fist full of flowers that I picked (actually stole) in the park that looked beautiful. Mam would love them.

The edges of the ice had melted but we jumped at the same time while I pulled my sister far enough to clear the soft edge of the ice. On the way back I had one hand full of flowers and with the other I held onto my sister ready to jump, so we could get home quick. We did not exactly jump at the same time and my sister was so tired by now, she was not used to going for long walks, that she did not even get off the ground. She fell onto the thin ice and started to scramble up but each time a piece of ice would break off and she was going deeper into the cold water while screaming her head off.

Reluctantly I put down my beautiful
flowers, jumped back onto the dirt and pulled
her out. She began to shiver. Her whole body
shook. I took all her clothes off and put my
sweater, coat, socks and shoes on her. I got
my flowers, rolled them in the wet clothes. I
carried my sister all the way, with the
flowers dangling on my back.

Unfortunately our visitors were still
there! When my sister saw my mother she
started crying all over again and told her I
had pushed her in! I never defended myself. I
was sure it would only make matters worse.
Besides my sister was so stupid, she could not
even jump 1/2 a meter. She walked too slow and
complained the entire time. I just wanted to
get some flowers for Mam and got stuck taking
her! So now that I had found a good excuse for
the problem I was at least at peace with
myself. I did not like the flowers anymore.
Mam had put them in a vase, but it bothered me
to look at them.

A few days later Pap said he believed
that it was an accident and I had been smart
to take off her wet clothes and put on dry

ones. He was sure that that was the reason she had not become ill.

I was also able to tell him that I practically froze on the way home, but I had not complained because Mam had already enough problems.

When Mam's bandages came off, her eyes looked better but her vision became progressively worse. For a while she alternated covering the left and right eye and then covered both eyes at night. She was very skinny, and when Robert was eight months old, she had to stop nursing him. He was a healthy, fat baby.

CHAPTER 25

LICE

Since Corrie had been there for several
months, everything went pretty smoothly and in
a certain routine, which Mam liked. The tub we
used to have wheat in had become our bathtub.
Mam put it in the middle of the entry hall on
our large coconut mat, heated water on the
stove and made sure that part of the house was
heated by firing up the kitchen stove.

Else was always first. According to Mam
she was never dirty. After she was done, Mam
put 2 extra buckets of hot water, then it was
my turn. Most of the time I was so dirty, she
made me soak until the water was cold.

I could never figure out how I got so
dirty. I just went to school and when school
was out at 4 P.M. I could play outside for 1
hour because I had to be ready at the table at
5 for dinner. So how dirty can you get? My
shoes were always dirty, too. I tried to avoid
the mud puddles, but sometimes I had to see

how deep they were: those things were important to know.

Complaints always came in multiples. Several parents in school had complained about me to my teacher. I recognized a lady from 2 1/2 blocks away. She was sitting in my teacher's office.
I knew what she was there for. I had rung her doorbell every day before and after school for weeks. Mrs. Godron made me apologize to her! Her last name was the same as mine. She was Pap's brother Johans' wife. But so what? I did not like her.

Mrs. Godron did not spill the beans when she realized my aunt did not know me. I appreciated that. Mrs.Godron and Pap got along well. He did a lot of counseling for problem children and helped in many other ways with the school's daily chores.

In the afternoon he went to school himself, an adult school called AVIO. We discussed what he learned - he knew I was always interested; there was a magic to it. My school was just a school: his was really learning something!

He often went on job interviews. Of course the job he had in the Hall of Records was not there any longer: he had burned the building down.

One Friday afternoon Mam had a total hissy-fit! When she was washing my sister's hair in that portable tub she discovered lice on her head. Not just a few, either; her head was covered. She send Pap to the doctor, who sent him directly to the pharmacy. He came home with liquid petroleum.

Mam heated the petroleum, put it on my sister's head, and covered it with a hot wet towel. While my sister was sitting on the kitchen chair, she did not waste any time with me. I had lice, too, and within minutes I was sitting there with my head in petroleum covered with a towel as well. I did not have as many, but the frenzy my mother was in it could have been only one and I got the treatment.

She did the same routine the next morning and Corrie was packing her things and moving out. She was the one that had brought lice into the house, and spending a lot more time with Else than me must have infested her more.

Days of combing with a special comb and picking eggs out of our hair eventually brought this to an end. Pap and I had to look for the eggs; Mam could not see them because her vision was so bad. I helped her clean out the room Corrie had stayed in. I had never seen that room so dirty.

I went with Mam for her regular check-up for her eyes. The doctor knew she was not getting enough rest at home so he ordered six weeks bed rest in the hospital. They also wanted to study her eye deterioration. Else and Robert went to a children's home and I stayed home with Pap. I went to school most of the day anyway!

We went to visit Mam every other day. It was an hour walking over and an hour back. Both her eyes were covered with bandages all the time. She was learning how to knit by feeling and she made for my sister and I a purse with a shoulder strap by weaving twine.

She wanted to see the baby, Robert, but every time Pap asked the doctor, they told him it was better not to. After six weeks they wanted her to stay longer, but she said she would not unless she saw the baby.

The day after she saw Robert, she was home. The roly-poly good looking baby boy was pale, skinny and had a rash so bad on his bottom it looked like dozens of small volcanoes. My mother was furious! My sister said that he cried every day and was never taken out of his crib. She had not even been allowed to give him his bottle after he had dropped it.

The homes were overloaded with children whose parents were wounded or just never came back. Not enough milk or food, not enough beds or rooms, and very few nurses or just help in general.

The first couple of days Mam cried a lot, and she had changed. She was not the strong person she used to be. Little things that did not bother her before became big problems. And she did not talk about things like she used to. In fact she just seemed to bury herself in work. She cleaned things that did not need cleaning, she yelled at me for things that happened long ago. Some of those things I had already forgotten.

Mam received more and better food coupons, more milk allowance, and extra coal.

We also received more money, which they spent wisely. One skein of yarn a week, turned into sweaters. Now I learned to knit to save Mam's eyes. I had to knit ten rows before dinner every day. During the war Pap was able to get food or trade one thing for another, but during these days there was nothing to get, nothing to trade.

I had not used my spot on the armchair in my own little corner for years, but once again I found myself sitting there knitting, counting stitches, and hurrying ten rows so I could eat:
bread soaked in warm milk for breakfast, eggs on bread for lunch, and brown beans and toast for dinner with oatmeal for dessert. For most people this was a lot better than wartime, but for us this was worse.

CHAPTER 26

EXTRA ELECTRA

It did not take Mam long to get Robert back in
shape and healthy again. He had a shade
darker hair like me and looked like Pap and I.
Else looked like Mam, their hair slightly
lighter and thicker.

Pap and I went to visit the famous
painter Dick van de Wedden across the street.
Pap was going to sell his paintings to make
extra money. With one arm he could not carry
the painting and ride the bike at the same
time, so he either had to walk or I had to go
along and hold the painting on the back of the
bicycle.

He sold a few here and there, but it was
not enough money for some of the things we
needed. Mam had made some new acquaintances,
but I thought Pap knew him already during the
war.

The electrician "Harry" came over once in
a while. He seemed to be more Mam's friend; he

often came over when Pap was not home. He was married. His wife was fat and lazy he told us, but I had never seen her nor had she come over to our house with him.

Pap went to visit a guy named Peter de Graaf. They always played chess for hours at a time. Peter's wife worked in an office somewhere. I went with Pap a few times to their house, but they did not like me because my language dialect was horrible and definitely below their standards. They suggested that Pap teach me proper Dutch instead of allowing me to speak that Jordaan slang.

When I was almost three, Mam had helped her brother who had an eel smokery in "De Jordaan." The smokery was downstairs and they lived upstairs. My uncle Bep and his wife had become very ill and Mam helped with the business for several months. Since this was the time I started to talk and could already put small sentences together, unfortunately I picked up that slang very quickly and it stuck with me. Another one of my mother's brothers said it was a disgrace to the whole family and how did they allow that in a Montessori School?

My teacher did not care. She said I would shed it sooner or later. Mam always tried to correct me or even make me say things over again. Pap did not even seem to notice and that was all that mattered to me. He did tell me one time to not say too much when we went to visit his psychology teacher, Mr. Baalder. But this teacher spoke with such sophistication that I could hardly understand him, anyway; and he sounded like a lady from a distance, so that did not count!

That section where Mam's brother had the eel smokery was adjacent to the red-light district and neither area had a good reputation. In the Jordaan people kind of did their own thing. They all had small businesses and worked very hard. It was kind of a town on its own in the middle of Amsterdam.

Pap was from the East of Holland so he had a dialect of his own; it just did not have a bad reputation like mine. Holland had elevem dialects of which some were very difficult to understand. East did not understand the West and North did not

understand the South. Very few people
traveled in those days so the dialect sections
stayed pretty tight.

Mam and Pap picked up government coupons
for food and clothing and a small amount of
cash for miscellaneous things on Wednesday.
One electric token per week was all we could
afford. Unfortunately we often, very often,
ran out of electricity on Sunday or Monday.

Pap went to school in the morning and he
had a part-time job for the government in the
afternoon. Mam complained constantly that she
hated running out of electricity all the time.
She also complained to Harry who had been
coming over a lot lately. Harry would do
anything for Mam; all she had to do was hint.
Harry was an electrician.

He pretended to like me, but I knew he
just needed to be on my good side. I felt he
was really just interested in Mam. He offered
to fix my skates, but I did not want him to
touch them. If he touched them I would
probably fall every five minutes the next time
I skated.

He was having tea with Mam one morning.
They were sitting across from each other at

the dining room table. He kept looking at her as if he owned her or as if he was possessed. Once in a while my psychology, learned so early in life, made me see and feel things I could not always explain. In fact the way he looked at Mam's every move made me feel uncomfortable. I began looking at him as potential trouble, and I watched him intensely, which in turn made him feel uncomfortable.

The arm of the easy chair, my own little corner, was a safe refuge and it gave me a clear view of the living and dining rooms.

I was messing with my knitting, Mam had just showed me a new stitch, and when I looked up he had his hand on Mam's. My breath stuck in my throat and I almost choked, but I kept quiet. He said she deserved better. Better what? I thought he said that now the war was over he was making good money.

So, why didn't he give her some? When Pap had money he bought Mam things, but he never talked about it! Mam said she could not take his offer. What about the children? Yah, what about us? Whatever good feelings I had left for Harry were now sour grapes, too, and the only other feeling I knew was hate. With this hate now came avoidance and very few words.

I thought about telling Pap what happened but I could handle this for him. I could keep an eye on Harry. So this became my new job, and I took all jobs seriously.

One afternoon I followed him home to his house and it was terrible. If he had all that money, why not fix his own house!
To my surprise Harry came over one late afternoon when Pap was home. They were looking in the closet of Robert's bedroom. The only thing in there was the electric meter on the wall. Pap and Harry were there a long time.

When they were done, there was a new electrical cord plugged into the wall socket and at the other end two bent wires connected onto the front of the meter. Not only did we have enough electricity all week long instead of three days, we did not need any coins at all.

Once every three months the token collector came to empty the meter. Mam still used one a week to not draw any suspicion.

The only problem was that this collector came unexpectedly at different times. This meant that Mam had to learn to take the cord off without getting shocked. Of course Harry showed Mam how to unhook the wires, thrn take out the plug and put two fuses back in that were on top of the meter ready at all times.

Once in a while someone would come to the door unexpectedly and the wire was undone before the door was opened. Getting caught would be a disaster. Stealing electricity is not the smartest thing to do, but when you have "war-ways" as we called them that seemed to excuse it. When you need it, take it.

Someone knocked. Mam opened the door, thinking it was her sister. As Pap came into the entry hall from the living room, a man with a dark blue suit and a badge was at the door. Pap turned around and looked straight at me. I knew what to do.

I slipped into the baby's room, pulled the wires, pulled the plug, screwed in the fuses, and then sat on the floor reorganizing the few toys Pap had made for my brother. The man came in, checked the meter and left.

"Good job, girl!", Pap said, putting his hand on my shoulder. "I knew you could do it." Mam cried. Her eyes got red and swollen. She kept yelling that "that was not a child's job, she could have been shocked."

Mam looked a little better at dinnertime. I felt 10 feet tall! Watching that Harry had paid off. I had watched Harry's every move when he showed Mam how to take those wires off without one touching the other, and make double sure YOU did not touch both wires at the same time ever!

Mam wanted to throw those connectors out, but when Monday came and our weekly token was used up, the connectors and cord were put in again.

CHAPTER 27

SLIPPERY DINNER

"Tante Annie is coming." We had not seen her in at least five years. She and her boyfriend were married somewhere in the North of Holland not far from where he had been hiding for all those years. My aunt worked close by and after work she would stay with him in a one-room storage shed on a farm.

She had lived with us before the war started and she took me everywhere, even on vacation. She had no children, and a niece was the next best thing.

She never complained about my mid-city language, as she called it. Instead she thought she had found a way to teach me to speak a more sophisticated Dutch through songs. We sang from morning till evening and the speech in the songs was perfect. Unfortunately the everyday language stayed the same.

Tante Annie and her husband Jan wanted to come back to Amsterdam to live. They needed to find a house and of course work. Before the war started my uncle worked in an insurance company.

When I woke up one morning Mam had already left. Both Mam and Pap had still a lot of outside business to tend to. Pap fed us breakfast. My sister ate very little, but I needed my time. I enjoyed every bite of my food! I could not figure out what my sister had against eating. I was always hungry and always ready to eat. Pap and I licked our plates. We could not let precious egg yolk or mashed potatoes go to waste. In fact we even had a special method. First the edges, then the ridge, then the middle.

Mam had been brought up more sophisticated, and did not like it, but she let it go with the excuse that we could not waste a crumb or a lick. This all started one day when Pap had trouble cleaning the last gravy off his plate with his fork. I sat next to him, to hold his plate and cut his meat, spread his butter etc. But when he was pushing hard to scrape the gravy off the plate it slipped out of my hand. He put his fork down, picked up his plate and licked it clean.

It was still morning when Mam came back with a gunny sack with eight large eel. She filled the kitchen sink with water and washed the eel. She let the water drain and washed them again.

She put a chair in front of the sink and told me to sit down and watch the eel to make sure they did not slither out of the sink onto the floor.

In amazement I watched those eel swim around in the sink. They were so big that the sink was pretty full. They were sliding every which way like a maze through the water. It was difficult to count them. I tried to count eight heads but I lost track, then eight tails, but that was really impossible.

I heard the front door open and close, then whispering voices. Who was that? Then the kitchen door opened all the way. It was Tante Annie. We hugged and kissed and stood there just looking at each other. "I came to sing songs," she said. "Do you remember that we sang songs together?" How could I forget? I loved that time and I loved to sing. "I sing

songs with Pap too," I told her, but that did
not seem to impress her.

When she looked past me she saw an eel
slide out of the sink onto the floor. We
hurried to pick it up. That thing was so big
and strong we had to hustle to hold onto it.
We each had a hold of an end and kind of threw
it back into the sink.

There followed lot of talking, laughing
and making plans. Aunt Annie had to see her
Dad immediately and she wanted Mam to go with
her. Pap was going on a job interview and
Uncle Jan left, too. I was sitting on the
chair again watching those eel for a second
time. Mam's last orders as she walked out the
door were, "Watch those eel for a few more
minutes. I'll be back shortly!" I was so
impressed that she took my sister. Watching
those eel or doing whatever else was more
pleasant any day!

I started the counting game again. First
the heads again. I thought I made it! I had
failed so many times that by the time I
counted eight of them, I thought I had really
accomplished something. Tails were impossible!
Maybe if I sat on the table behind me. Now I

was a little higher up and I could see the whole sink. I was getting tired, I wanted to go to sleep, or maybe just close my eyes a minute. Oh, this was terribly boring! Then it hit me: Mam and Tante Annie were going all the way to Opa Happe, on the other side of the harbor. The last time Mam and I went it had taken four hours!

I was not going to sit there for four hours, was I? Yes, I was! Maybe they were meeting somewhere else. I tried to think of all the songs I used to sing with Tante Annie, but that even became boring. I slouched down into the chair, then sat up again, then back on top of the table, but boredom got the better of me and I dozed off.

I woke up scared and frantically started counting the eel. Seven, then seven again; one was missing! I looked on the floor but no sign of water or an eel. I counted again and this time there were eight. Finally I calmed down, when something caught my eye. There was a movement in the crack where the sink had sagged away from the counter. The crack in the corner was at least 1-1/2 inches wide.

I sat real still and kept my eyes glued
to the darkness in the crack. There it was
again, something shiny. Instantly I knew it
was a rat. I wondered if a rat would eat a
live eel. Of course rats eat eel. They eat
anything and everything. They would eat me
too if they got a chance! I had seen rats
come through the crack before; there was
plenty of room for a big one to squeeze
through.

I looked around to see if there was
anything I could put in the crack. The only
thing I saw was a towel. Mam would kill me if
I used that. It was the only towel we had for
the whole family. Four people to one towel.

While I looked away the rat had stuck his
head through the corner hole and two eel fell
onto the floor. They must have seen him
coming too.

Now I had double trouble. I had to bend
over and pick up a slippery eel and watch the
rat at the same time.

I grabbed a wooden spoon and hit the sink
corner, then quickly picked up one slimy,
wiggly, strong eel and threw it back into the

sink. At least I had one now. The other eel had slithered to the back door.

I made several attempts to hit the sink corner and go for the eel, but I could not do it fast enough. That rat seemed to know exactly what I was doing. The minute I looked away he would make another attack.

I saw my sister's doll on the other side of the door just inside the hall. I grabbed it and sat the doll on the table and focused the eyes on the corner of the crack. The rat stayed back and I picked up the other eel and threw it back in the sink too.

Pap came home first and I showed him what I had done. He studied the situation for a moment and said that I had the light of the window reflect into the doll's eyes and that must have made the doll look alive so the rat stayed put. "Pretty clever," Pap said. "Pretty clever!"

I heard him tell the incident to Mam and my Aunt and Uncle that evening, but nobody seemed impressed. Pap having only one arm always had to think of better ways to do things. What was easy for others with two hands was for Pap a challenge with only one.

"I don't need a right arm. That's why I have you! You have a brain. All you have to do is use it. Don't waste it!" Pap said. "No" is not acceptable. You fight until you find a solution! Never give up!

Pap liked me as a student. I enjoyed solving problems especially when no one else could. But most of the time no one tried! Also Pap made a big deal out of it every time I did something special, and for me that was the best reward.

Mam had steamed the eel in the double boiler. She made a mustard sauce and I was too busy eating to hear all of the conversation at the dinner table. I did hear that Tante Annie was going to rent a house just a few blocks away. "You come and see me often," she said.

She was a nice lady. Her new husband looked old enough to be her father. I tried to guess how old he was. He had to be older than Pap. Maybe the war had made him old. He was very quiet too. I knew he worked in an office. So did the neighbor upstairs and he was quiet too. Maybe offices were like schools, so they were not allowed to talk a lot. Maybe that made them quiet and serious.

CHAPTER 28

IT PAYS TO HAVE FRIENDS

Mam, my sister, and I had lunch. Mam had fried
potatoes and we could only have one slice of
bread. The potatoes were at least a year old
and pretty dried out, so frying was the best.
Our ration was one loaf of bread a week for
the four of us, and Mam would bake one more
loaf, and of course we had cheese.

Nobody came or was invited to come and
eat those days. We had to be careful not to
run out ourselves. Pap's lunch was waiting
for him on the back of the pipe of the
potbelly stove, to keep it warm.

Mam became worried when a few hours had
gone by and he was not home yet. She started
singing to cover up her nervousness and her
feelings. She sang a lot but her intense
housecleaning gave her away. The vacuum
cleaner running and Mam singing at the same
time was a regular sound now.

At those times Mam totally ignored me and I would retreat to the arm of the easy chair in my own little corner, wondering what Pap had done this time. He had been late before, in fact many times, and besides he had said he would be back. Maybe he would be back in a few days: that had happened before, too. When Pap said he would be back that was good enough for me!

I looked in the kitchen to see if his bicycle was there and it was, so he could not be very far. Mam and Pap had whispered a lot yesterday, but that had probably been about me. Mam did not like it that Pap always took me with him. But what better decoy could he have?

I heard footsteps outside the window. I could not see who it was, but it sounded familiar. The door opened. Thank God it was Pap. He looked funny, something was wrong.

He was as white as a ghost, his face looked scared and hisupper body was leaning forward. Mam closed the front door. I heard it lock and then I could not believe what I saw! Pap and Mam were hugging each other in the entry hall as if they were holding each other up! What happened to being strong, I thought. Mam had tears in her eyes and Pap kept saying, "Oh, my God, oh, my God!"

He finally noticed me over Mam's shoulder and came over to me. He took my hand and pulled me into the living room. "Turn around," he said. Then he put his arm around my waist and lifted me up. He used to do that when I was little. I had almost forgotten how that felt, but right away it felt comfortable.

"Riek," he said, "Come over here, I'll tell you what happened."

Mam brought his lunch and my sister and we sat around the round table. Pap took a deep breath and after a few bites of food he looked out the window with a faraway look. Then he told us the story.

"I went with Peter (his chess playing partner) to the bunker next to the railroad. One of the coalmen on the train had promised to throw out some coal for us at a certain spot. We could use some heat here you know!

"We were supposed to be just past the bunker but it turned out to be a little farther. One hundred yards past the bunker Peter turned back, but I kept going.

"I had my gunny sack half full. I saw several army boots in front of me. I stood up and looked directly into three gun barrels. Three German soldiers stood there and asked me what I was doing there.

"The officer in the middle recognized me and I recognized him. I had taken his wife out of Germany at least two years ago. He started yelling at me 'Don't you know that you are not supposed to be here! Get out of here and never come back!'

"'Why don't we just shoot him?"' asked one of the others. 'No!' he yelled even louder. 'This guy is worthless!' He motioned with his rifle for me to go. I walked a few steps and then started running. 'Make sure you never come back here again, stupid!'

"He knew who I was, and he saved my life. This is as close as I have come, yet. He even fired the gun in the air while I was passing the bunker. I sure thought I was a goner!

"This officer surprised the other two by yelling at me and that split second saved my life. They never ask questions, they are supposed to just shoot." Pap was still pale and shaking. He even hit his teeth with his

fork trying to eat his fried potatoes. his
favorite.

He did not go anywhere for a few days,
but after a brief conversation with Heemo
while we were on a short walk, he had work to
do again.

Every day we walked to different places
some I had been before, some I had not. There
had been bombing in Rotterdam and everyone
worried that Amsterdam would be next, maybe
the Eastern part of the city.

Pap was a good strong link in the chain.
He always did what he was asked to do
regardless of the danger involved. Somehow I
felt important when I was with him. I did not
think of myself as a decoy; I was a real help.
Pap even told me so!

I was tired at night after keeping up
with Pap's big steps all day and sleeping was
not a problem. But I woke up in the middle of
the night; it was too quiet! I went to check
on Mam and Pap and they were not in bed. Just
as I finished on the toilet Mam came up out of
the cellar. Her eyes were red, she had been
crying.

They had heard on the radio that the other side of the harbor had been bombed. Mam's father, stepmother and her brother Henk lived there.

We left as soon as it was daylight. This was one of the few times I saw Mam and Pap go together. Many people did not know they belonged together.

They assumed that the Fokker Factory had been the target, but that was farther North. The warnings had been for the East part of Amsterdam. The radio information from England was usually accurate.

We walked as far as the central station when Pap went ahead and told us to wait right there for 1/2 an hour. If he was not back by then we were to leave and go home. He looked Mam straight in the eye and repeated, "Go home if I am not back in 1/2 an hour!"

Pap crossed the street, first went to the left, then changed his mind and went to the right, and then disappeared around the corner of the station.

Mam did not just stand still. She walked up and down the sidewalk. Pap came back very shortly and motioned us to walk back. He took my hand and walked fast in front of Mam and the baby buggy. Boy, she could maneuver that thing! My sister had outgrown that two years earlier, but it was Mam's trademark so she could not give it up. She had radios and medicines to deliver.

It took us over an hour to get home, half the time of going over. I was exhausted. Mam and Pap did not talk after they opened the door. Pap motioned us to be quiet and stay in the entry hall. He tip-toed from room to room as if he expected someone to be in there. As he opened each door cautiously and waited, he kept shaking his head "no."

But someone had been there. The front door was unlocked when Mam put the key in. They never left the door unlocked.

Mam started looking around to see if something was missing, but everything seemed to be there. They looked for clues until we went to bed; they whispered until they went to bed; everything that normally happened became a problem. My sister was not allowed to cry. I could not go into the backyard. Even the cat had to stay in.

We woke up in the middle of the night to a loud explosion that rocked the whole house. The windows rattled so hard it is a wonder that they did not break. Some were still boarded up from the last time, which was about three years before.

Again Mam and Pap searched the whole house. They tried to put the unlocked door together with the explosion but nothing worked out to a solution. They never found out who was in the house that day, but a few days later Mam discovered that the heavy glass table cover on the table in the living room had split in half. That had been the explosion!

CHAPTER 29

NERVOUS BREAKDOWN

Mam became more nervous as time went by. Too
many things were happening that played with
her emotions. Mam cried a lot. I knew she
was not strong anymore. One day she lost her
bread knife and she cried all day. Sometimes
when she cried I had to hide because it made
me cry too.

I also cried when we sang a song about a
"little lost lamb" in a large meadow crying
for his mother. I hated that song because it
made me cry, yet I could not cover my ears
because I wanted to hear. Were we all
beginning to break down? Maybe I was playing
with my own emotions, or maybe I just wanted
an excuse to cry too.

I came home from school one day and Mam
was in bed. The bed had been moved into the
front bedroom. I walked in quietly and sat on
the edge of the bed. Mam was shaking all over.

She was shaking so hard it made the bed vibrate.

Pap came in and said the doctor was coming and I was to help with my sister. He also wanted me to help with Mam. "She needs someone there all the time."

I heard the doctor tell Pap that she had a breakdown. Pap made arrangements with the doctor to come every other day unless Mam got worse. He would give the doctor 1/2 pound of wheat for each visit. Where was he going to get that, we only had a little wheat left?

After the doctor left Pap made a hot water bottle and we ate bread in warm milk, with sugar and butter. I buttered 2 slices for each of us and one for my sister, put a little sugar on that and than poured the warm milk over the bread. Boy, that was good!

Pap explained to me that Mam's nervous system had been overloaded. Too many things had happened and she needed time to get over this. Her eyes needed rest again. Mam needed vitamins and iron. She often started sentences like, "One day, when I can't see any longer....

A few days later when my sister was taking a nap, Pap told Mam that he and I were going for a short walk. When we got to the corner he became very serious. He began explaining to me how to steal fruit from the store. "No one can buy it, there is no money, we just as well use it."

He showed me how to crawl to the wooden crates and just reach my hand around and take only one at a time. He said he was too big. "Even when I am on my hands and knees my back shows above the edges of the crates. You are short enough to stay under the height of the crate." The first time I was shaking and my heart pounded all the way home.

Mam ate that apple and smiled. If she only knew, but I promised Pap I would never tell her. She had enough problems without this. The second time it was a little easier and as I did it every day I became aware of my surroundings and became more at ease, which Pap said was safer. "Don't ever take anything unless you really need it," he said, "like Mam right now has to have that. Always be careful. Never be in a hurry. Haste makes waste!"

This was the beginning of our secrets that even Mam did not know about, the beginning of a time that made me feel grown up, important and very close to Pap.

After a few weeks I knew every crate of fruit and vegetable in that market. There was not a lot. Food was still scarce, but whatever there was I got some of it. I went back to the farmer and stole cucumbers. I stole eggs from a backyard chicken coop.

Mam started getting better, but her recovery took a long time. The word 'stealing' was never used. Pap said, "Nobody helps you during these bad times. You have to help yourself. A lion does not kill unless he is hungry. Getting food this way is not fun, but has become a necessity; therefore you have my permission. If you get caught tell them I told you to do it!"

Mam never asked where the fruit came from. She thought Pap bought it for her. That was fine with me. At least I did not have to explain anything.

Pap and I went to visit his brother's wife one day. His brother was in Germany. Pap said he was going to be gone just a few

minutes and while he was gone I stole a
bicycle inner tube for his bicycle. Good
thing this was not close to home or someone
might have noticed him back on the bicycle
after a long time of just walking. He never
said thank you, but he did say how much time I
saved him now that he could run errands on the
bike.

I did notice some of the things Pap
brought home. I knew some of that was stolen,
too. I never opened my mouth though, but a
wink from Pap let me know I was right.

CHAPTER 30

A TANKER RIDE

The Canadian soldiers were bringing supplies in in large tankers, and since one of the big garage's entrance was just across the street, I walked over to see what they were doing.

Every day big crates and large boxes were unloaded. Then the crates were opened and were reloaded into smaller trucks which delivered the food to the distribution centers throughout the city; the medical supplies were delivered to the hospitals.

One morning as I was leaning against the wall of the garage watching them work, one of the soldiers came over and asked my name. My breath stuck in my chest and it made me stutter. The last time one of the German soldiers in that garage had spoken to me, he had taken my puppy.

"You want a ride?" "Where to?" I asked. "This load goes to the end of the Ferdinand

Boll street. Not too far. Ten minutes," he
said.

He did not wait for me to answer. He
pushed me up into the huge tanker, walked
around and got in on the other end and started
the engine! The whole thing shook and it was
so loud and the seats were big. Going out of
the garage I could see down on everyone from
way up there. I had always looked up to
people. I was still little and this was the
first time I could see down on them. What a
good feeling! That monster was so big we could
not go very fast which was fine with me, I
enjoyed every moment of that ride.

While men were unloading the boxes I took
a good look at the steering wheel, the big
pedals and all the knobs. The windows were
dirty, the seat the Canadian soldier had sat
on was shiny. It scared me when the soldier
came to my side of the truck and asked me if I
wanted to drive one of these?

He went around again, sat in the driver's
seat and gave me a piece of gum. I had never
seen gum before so I put it in my pocket. I
did not know it was edible.

On the back of the truck was a canvas. They had rolled it back and fastened to the back of the cab.

Hey, are you going back to the garage? Take #67 instead. We don't have room for it over here – it belongs over there. The soldier motioned me to come out of the truck. "We have to take that thing back over there," he said, pointing at this huge tanker. It had neither a front nor back and there were no wheels, only steel bands, that roll over to make it move. We stood up in the center even though there were chairs to sit on, but standing up we could see out. Now this was really high up!

We started going and I did not know if we were going forward or backwards but when we made a turn I knew we were not going back the way we had come! I had to get home! I had not told anyone that I was going somewhere. Mam would be furious. The least she would do was kill me! The soldier must have sensed my concern and he said that we were just going for a short ride and then home.

Around the corner was a sandy area in front of one of the canals. On the outskirts of the city the edges of the canals were not always walled off like in the center of Amsterdam. He pulled a lever and we drove over the sandy area straight into the water. It was an amphibian tanker and could go into the water, too. We had sat down in the seats and when I looked out of the window we were totally surrounded with water.

He made a loop in the water and went back onto the sand again. He had switched the lever back. I was so excited. I had never seen anything like this before and I was actually on it! "If you like a ride again one day you can come over anytime!"

I ran back home and took a deep breath before I opened the door. I kept my face calm, but inside I was so excited. That was really something: we drove into the water and out again!

Mam was busy with my sister and there really seemed no opportunity to tell her where I had been and what I had done. Pap was not home so I conveniently tried to forget about it, but every time I put my hand in my pocket I felt that piece of gum. Instantly it brought back the excitement of that ride.

On the arm of that chair in my little corner I relived the experience over and over while holding that gum in my hand in my pocket. I unwrapped it and licked it. It tasted sweet, but I had better wait for Pap to make sure it was edible. I rewrapped it. I wrapped and rewrapped it so many times the paper was wrinkled and I had to smooth it out.

After I had time to think about the things I did, I made up my mind not to tell Mam. She became so nervous and upset over little things, this would probably really set her off. Maybe she would start shaking again, and we had to worry about her eyes. No, it was better to keep my mouth shut.

Pap came home from school that afternoon frustrated. "Why do I have to learn to sew on a commercial sewing machine? Many people with two hands cannot do that."

The only jobs starting up were in the clothing manufacturing industry, but for Pap with one arm, it was a difficult job. The government assigned what they wanted and it was up to you to do it. He also started taking sewing machine mechanics classes, but that was just as difficult! I asked him if I

could go with him. I always helped him
before, but he said kids were not allowed on
his job. Not many people had a child to help a
parent. A lady had had her fingers caught in
one of those machines one day and when Pap was
telling the story to Mam I thought that that
better not happen to Pap. He had only one
hand left to begin with, so if something
happened to that arm what would he do then?

I had found a new way of getting meat. My
big cat Pimmy came home one day with a big
roast. I had plenty of time to figure out
where he got that. Pap was in school and at
work all day so I had many hours to myself.

Sitting in a corner of the yard I watched
the cat for hours. I began to see a pattern in
his every day run around. There was a robin
nest in a cedar tree two back yards over. He
checked on that every day. He also watched
the upstairs balcony. I could not determine
exactly which floor. I had never paid much
attention what the neighbors did on the
balconies upstairs.

Every other week we got a meat ration,1/4
pound per person. It came frozen from Canada.
I watched the cat notice a paper on the edge

of the 2nd floor balcony railing one day. As soon as he saw it he started climbing up the drainpipe. When he reached the balcony he walked on the railing and pushed the package off. It fell straight down and landed with a thud about four feet away from our back door.

I did not move until he was all the way down and then I picked up the meat. I tore off several pieces for him and brought the rest in the house. Mam cut the meat into small pieces and made soup that day. When Pap came home and heard the story he looked me straight in the eyes: "Don't you climb that pipe, it will not hold you!"

There was no need for me or Pimmy to climb the pipe. The people never put meat there again to thaw out.

CHAPTER 31

NEIGHBOR WATCHING

Across the backyards were, of course, the
balconies of the houses from the next street
over. Sitting with my back against the wall
outside under the dining room window I could
see several straight across from the back
yards. Some people would hang wash on lines,
some had coal in the coal shed on the enc, and
one even had little birds in a flight cage.

I had to saw some firewood every day.
Mam got too tired, and Pap was working and in
school, so I needed exercis, at least that is
what Mam said. Pap had told me I was too
strong for a girl. But whatever the reason I
got stuck doing that job.

I would get so tired that I would have to
rest. I did not like to rest because that took
even more time. In the beginning it was a fun
job. Pap and I had done it together each on
one end of the saw. Just by myself it became
boring and tiresome. I had to rest.

I saw two men leaning on the railing of
the balcony on the other side. Even though I
could lipread very well, they were too far
away to see what they were saying. The way
their heads were moving and their hands were
gesturing it must have been an interesting
conversation.

Since they had now drawn my attention I
would look every time I sat down to rest to
see if they were there. Some days I would see
the one guy, some days the other, sometimes
nobody. All the watching I had done with Pap
to see how people acted and moved made me keep
on looking for them.

Many weeks later, it was a better day
because the sun would come out once in while.
I sat against the wall soaking up the sun.
When a cloud would come in front of the sun I
would hurry up and saw some more.

As I looked up I saw the same two guys
leaning on the balcony edge. This time the one
had his arm over the shoulder of the other. I
crept slowly like a cat along the fence to the
chicken coop so I could get a closer look. I
looked through a slit in the fence and could
now see them clearly. One kissed the other and

then they were holding hands. I had never seen two men so friendly before so I kept on looking. I was such a nosy little shit!

Then they embraced each other and kissed on the mouth. I had never seen that before! I had Pap seen embrace Heemo after a close call or when people returned from Germany or England they hugged each other, but I had never seen them kiss like that!

The next few weeks I watched a lot and the wood sawing was not so boring, but I never saw much more of that kissing. Once in a while I saw a carpet over the railing or one of them would water the geraniums they had in a planter.

Pap was talking to Mam's friend Harry on the corner when I saw the guy walk by. I turned my face toward Pap's legs so he could not see my face, but when I watched him walk away from us he was walking like a lady, his hips swinging from side to side. I watched him until he disappeared in his front door. Pap was busy talking to Harry, so I had to wait, but I was definitely going to ask him about those two.

My sister had started kindergarten and was very well liked by everyone. She was good looking, always smiled and had many, many friends. She had mostly girls as friends, I had mostly boys as friends.

Mam worried a lot about my sister, so when she started school I was responsible for her again. If there were any problems (usually her fault) it was my job to fix them. So I made it clear from the beginning whomever touched her, argued with her, or hit her would have to deal with me. My reputation was not that good anyhow.

Mam had bought some beads which my sister had made a necklace of and was showing it around to everybody. In an argument over a top that you spin on the pavement a boy pulled her necklace and broke it. The beads were all over the street. One of Else's friends came to tell me, so I beat him up good. His mother came to school with him the next day and showed my teacher all his black and blue marks, scrapes and black eye. I was expelled for the rest of the week, which was three days.

Pap never reprimanded me. He did say that I came short of killing the kid and that was a little too much. "Next time maybe a little less would do."

On one afternoon when he came home from work early he helped me saw firewood, and when it was time to rest I made him sit next to me under the window. I pointed to the balcony across the yards.

I told him the whole story. He just looked at me and said, "You are a smart little shit, too smart for your age."

All people are different. We could not live in this world if we were all the same. If you really think you hate someone or dislike someone, try to find one good thing in that person and then you can very often except them the way they are.

Pap said to me one day, "I need your help again in the next few weeks. You have to help Mam with shopping. Her eyes are getting worse and I am getting an extra job. It has to be a secret, because if they catch me, we lose everything."

It had been a long time since Pap really needed me. I did not care what I had to do as long as I could spend more time with him.

CHAPTER 32

THE NEWSPAPER ROUTE

When Pap had said he needed my help I thought
I would be spending more time with him but
that turned out to be less.

He began delivering newspapers after his
regular job. All the work people did was
contracted by the government except a few
minor employment such as newspaper deliveries.
Pap's job in the garment industry was paid for
and run by the government, so the newspaper
job was extra money not reported. And a
second job was definitely not allowed.

His route included the streets around the
park. He delivered the paper between 5 and 6
P.M. I would stand on each corner ahead of
him and watch if a suspicious person would be
watching Pap. The job was exciting at first
but after a few months when it got really cold
it became boring. It was a very busy time. To
school during the day, then help Pap, then
dinner and to bed. Mam rented the living room

to a nice lady. My sister and I called her
Tante Cisca. She had an electric sewing
machine and she sewed all day long. Prrrrrt.
Prrrrrrt. You could hear that machine until
late in the evening.

Just as Pap figured his paper route was
pretty safe, we noticed a guy by the park
entrance two days in a row. When Pap went up
the stairs to deliver the paper I ran up
behind him and told him about the man
watching.

Pap dropped his large bag at the top of
the stairs and went down to take a look. Sure
enough the guy looked Pap straight in the eye.

Pap took me by the hand and we walked up
and down the block and then up the stairs
again. Pap knocked on the door and asked the
lady who opened it if he could leave his bag
there while he ran an errand. When we came
down the stairs we saw the man still standing
at the park entrance. We walked toward home,
but he knew he had been caught. All the man
had to do was to call the newspaper office.

Pap quit that day, but they withheld a
portion of the money each week to repay what
he had made delivering newspapers. So now we

had even less than what Pap said was not enough. Pap paced the floor in the dining room a lot back and forth....back and forth.... figuring out how to make extra money. Pap was a good salesman but there was nothing to sell. The goods were just beginning to come into the country, but it would take years before things could be running smooth. Most people were like us: no money, just simple necessities.

Mam lived in a state of panic 24 hours a day. The income from the rented room was a no-no too, and we still had the electrical wire, getting electricity without paying. With Pap gone all day to work and me in school, Mam was responsible all day.

The winter was coming and Mam spent days and weeks going from agency to agency with her coupons to get blankets, clothes and food. Every place she had to wait many hours in line.

We did not spend a lot of time together in those days. Mam had Robbie as a baby, I was stuck with my sister in school, and Pap worked, went to school and spent a lot of time away from home.

Pap came home with a big smile on his face one day, actually it was a big smirk! I had planned to tell him that I did not like the big armchair where it was. When Mam rented out the living room the chair was put by the stove in the dining room. There were too many people walking by all the time. I wanted to do my knitting, thinking, planning, and reading in a more quiet place. But I did not have a chance to talk with him.

Pap had brought meat, bread, rice, potatoes, and butter; his bicycle was loaded. I thought that he had gone to a farmer but he had not been gone long enough for that. He had come home very late several nights; in fact, I had not heard him come home. I always tried to stay awake and wait for him but I always fell asleep.

I went to bed later and later. I was helping Mam count rows and stitches on her knitting. Her eyes were getting worse by the day. Now that the government provided medical services Mam could go to an eye specialist every Tuesday.

Pap fried the meat, Mam cooked potatoes and I ground the wheat in the coffee grinder.

No wonder my arms were so strong: I was the only one in school who could do 10 push-ups in P.E. Pap had met a lady named Susanna who paid him to run errands and do chores. She drank a lot of liquor, Pap said, and she often paid more money than he actually had earned.

We were all excited with the food and extra riches. Mam had just received 4 coupons for 4 wool blankets. My sister and I got a light green one, Mam and Pap had a blue one, and the baby had a pink even though Robbie was obviously a boy.

I hardly saw Pap anymore. The daily routines became so boring that I began to look for trouble in school. I had become friends with a girl named Else Visser. One day I walked to her house with her after school. I invited her to go swimming with me on Thursday evenings, but she had to bring a parent. Her father came with her the first Thursday. Mr. Visser looked like a bully. In fact, he looked like Popeye's life long enemy Brutus.

I loved to swim and now I had a friend to swim with. I liked the ride home too. Pap and Mr.Visser on the bicycles and Else and I on the back hiding behind their bodies from the wind. Even though Mr.Visser was big and looked mean, he seemed to have an insecurity. Of course I am just a kid, I could be wrong.

I had never seen Else's mother before until I walked her home one day and she was waiting on the step in front of the house. Else became very nervous when she saw her mother. Mrs. Visser was standing there with her hands on her hips and when we were within a few feet of her all hell broke loose!

"Where is the button?" she screamed. "I told you not to come home without it!" Else had lost a button from her dress, and of course nobody made or sold buttons. The only buttons available were the ones of old dresses from grandmothers and aunts. It was a small round button she had lost and we looked for hours and never found it.

Else came to school with swollen eyes the next morning. She whispered that they had taken turns beating her and had thrown her down the stairs. She showed me some of her bruises and on her back she had at least 20 belt streaks. I could not believe my eyes - I had never seen anything like that. She could not go swimming because she was hurting all over. I watched her at school for days. She began to move better and better as the days went by. She never complained.

I had had spankings before, and some were pretty good, but I had never seen someone so beat up before over a little button.
This was the first time I actually saw and witnessed the interaction in another family. This was the first time I saw that others had less, a lot less, than we did.

Pap and Mr. Visser talked when Else and I swam on Thursday nights. They dried us off when we were shivering and we rode home on the back of their bicycles. Pap said that Mr. Visser had unrealistic ideas. One time I was invited into their house. I was afraid to sit down. They did not have much, but what they had was polished and very, very clean.

They did not have bed. They slept on the floor. I thought all people had beds. That was also the first time I saw Else's little sister. had almost forgotten that she existed because Else hardly ever talked about her.

Well, everyone knew I had a little sister! God forbid all the trouble she

caused! Even though I felt sorry for Else
Visser I thought she was lucky to not be
responsible for her sister. On the way home
from swimming one Thursday, Pap and Mr. Visser
did not speak a lot. I was always so cold that
I would push myself against Pap's back. When
he talked to Mr. Visser I could hear that
through his body. It made me feel good to be
so close. I might not otherwise have noticed
that they did not speak a lot.

When we split ways and we made a right
turn into our street and they went straight
Pap said that Mr. Visser did not like us. Pap
had not agreed with him on something and I had
become a bad influence on his daughter in
school.

I finally told Pap about the beating Else
had had a few months ago. Pap wished I had
told him earlier but it did not matter anymore
anyway.

The Vissers pulled Else out of school and
put her in the 6th Montessori school, which
was actually closer than my school. I did not
see Else but a few times after that. Many
months later she was waiting for me at the

corner of my street and told me she was moving
to Russia.

She was very nervous and had changed. She
looked scared and timid even though she was
big in size for her age. She grabbed both of
my hands and said, "You are the best friend I
ever had. Even though I did not see you for a
long time I thought about you every day. I
missed our Thursday swimming and our games at
school. Maybe someday I will be happy like
you. I like to be different from what I am and
I don't want to be like my parents."

Else could not explain how her parents
were but she did understand that that was not
what she wanted. The rough childhood showed on
her face and reflected in her voice. She
should have Pap for a father, "I thought."
But I did not want to share him.

Else did not want to leave me and she had
thought about running away, but just thinking
about that made her scared. She had only gone
to school and back home again. No swimming, no
friends, no visitors, and no recreation. I
asked her if she thought that it would change
when they went to Russia, but she did not
think so.

Hand in hand we walked towards her house. We figured she was at least 45 minutes late. Her punishment would be 45 hits with the belt, one for every minute. "I can handle that," she said "I had to say goodbye to you. You are the only friend I ever had."

I turned around when she ran for home. Running could save her one minute.

I stuck to Pap like glue. I made him explain to me why Else and her parents were living like that. Mr. Visser dictated his family and the only way to maintain this strict discipline was though extremes. I still did not understand why that big man had to beat a little girl to maintain order. I could not remember that she had ever done anything wrong besides lose a little button.

Pap and I walked by her house weeks later and the house was empty. I held Pap's hand real tight and even leaned for security; Else had left a lasting impression on me.

CHAPTER 33

PAP'S FRIEND SUSANNA

Pap graduated from the Avio College with honors. It did not change his working situation but his early evenings were now free. Sometimes he would pick me up from school and we would walk home together. It was like old times except the walks were shorter. Since my friend Else moved to Russia I had become interested in other family situations.

I asked Pap so many questions that he finally gave me a book to read. I read every spare minute I had. I read about relationships between parents, parents and children, children and animals etc. I began to understand about the need people have to rule others. Leaders and followers amongst adults and children. The more I read the more I wanted to know.

One day I decided to try my teachers patience to the limit. She really liked me.

In fact some kids thought I was the teacher's pet.

After recess I went home instead of going back to class just to see what would happen. The next morning she sent me to her office where I was to wait for her; she would be in there shortly.

While I was sitting there I looked around and everything was so orderly. She had a lot of books and even a telephone. I read the book titles: child psychology, child discipline, child behavior. I looked back at the phone. I picked up the receiver but I heard nothing. I figured the thing was probably broken.

I heard her coming down the hall and open the door. She sat behind her desk in front of me. "Where did you go yesterday after recess?" she asked. "Home, just home," I said. "Don't you like school anymore?" "I love school," I heard myself say, but I was thinking that it was boring lately.

"You come to class 1/2 hour early four days in a row to make up the four hours you missed yesterday. Do you understand? I need to see your Dad, so ask him to come and see me." She did not wait for me to answer. She just left me sitting there. When morning recess came she told me to go into the classroom.

The next morning I was at school at 8:30, but there was no teacher in sight. She showed up around 8:55. She did not excuse being late, but just opened the door and sent me into the classroom.

The second morning, I was there again at 8:30 and again no teacher. I was waiting when I noticed a police car driving fast with the lights on toward the police station. I decided to go out to see what was happening.

I was drawn over into the direction of the station. There were two old policemen standing at the corner who would not let me go any further.

I was waiting to see if anything was going to happen that was interesting when the policeman asked me where I was going to school. I pointed into the direction of my school. "The Montessori School?" he asked. "Yes," I answered very politely. "You look familiar," the other policeman said. "Me? You mean, me?" "Are you related to Bertus van Voorst?" "Yes, how do you know?" I asked.

"You look just like him. I hope you are not
as much trouble as he used to be. Are you a
runaway too?"

I got back to school at 9 A.M. Boy, that
teacher was mad. "Where were you? I told you
to come early at 8:30, remember?" I allowed
her to assume I was not there at all.

Pap had to come with me the next morning.
We were there at 8:30 and she did not show
until 8:50. She started being real weird to
Pap: "I have an old mother to take care of in
the morning, so that is why I am late," she
whined. Well, don't tell me to come at 8:30,
I thought. She and Pap talked about the class,
her limited time and I heard him tell her
something about me changing. She also said I
had had two fights. She was lying to Pap.
There had been four fights and none were my
fault. Two with the new kid, who said his
parents were rich, and two fights over my
sister. Which ones should he not know about?

Pap went into the classroom and gave a
speech to the whole class about being good and
doing our work the way we did in the beginning
of the year. The teacher had an old mother to
take care of and we had to be nice to her and

appreciate her for all she did for us. He
reminded us that she had a classroom and she
was principal at the same time and that was a
lot of work and responsibility.

The children liked Pap and they promised
to be better.
I had really liked that teacher but something
had changed, all right, and it was not me. She
started calling me Ans instead of Ansje. Had
I grown up all of a sudden or something?

Pap and I learned the times tables while
on our walks. In walking rhythm I learned them
quickly. The teacher did not know I knew them
until the upper graders had a test and I knew
them better than they did. I seemed to
surprise her but not please her, but that was
all right. I did not need her - I had Pap.

On Saturday morning Pap took me with him
to meet his lady boss, whom he ran errands
for. We came to a hotel and took an elevator
to the second floor. I had never been in an
elevator before. Pap greeted the old man
sitting on a stool in the corner pushing the
levers that operated that ugly big box. Pap
said it was better than walking so I took his
word for it. I wondered how many people lived

in the building. The long hallway had many doors all the same colors gray. The walls were gray too. It looked ugly. I could not help but wonder how Pap had found that lady here out in nowhere.

Pap knocked and opened the door. There were four rooms: living room, two bedrooms, and a very small kitchen. The kitchen looked more like a closet. "Is that you Bert?" a woman's voice called. "Jah, it's me, I want you to meet my daughter." "Oh, come in I'd love to." We walked into a messy bedroom, clothes everywhere, a tray with liquor bottles on the dresser, and she was still in bed.

When she lifted her arm from under the blanket I saw that she was naked. How could she invite us in when she was still in bed and what was she doing naked?

And her hair! My God it looked like a witch's wig! "Bert, order some breakfast for us and I will dress quickly," she said.

I walked behind Pap into the living room. He pushed a button on a little black box and ordered enough breakfast for an army. This woman came out in a robe but she had not buttoned the front. She had just folded one side over the other and tied a belt around it. When she sat down in the chair you could see her whole naked body. She saw me look at her and fixed it somewhat and turned towards Pap so I did not have a direct look.

What a strange lady I thought and such a mess everywhere. "The children are at my mother's," she said to Pap. I realized Pap should not have brought me. She had made plans and that had not included me.

What kind of 'work' was this anyway? Mam never walked around like that. When the breakfast came I wondered who had done all the cooking and so quickly. I ate a lot, and Pap kept shoving me more. The lady gave Pap a hundred dollar bill. I had not seen the new version since the war ended.

She made a list and Pap and I went to the store. She must have bathed while we were gone. She was dressed very nicely, and with her hair combed she looked a lot better.

"I am going with my mother and children to the Zoo this afternoon. Do you and Ans want to come?" "She has swimming on Saturday afternoon," Pap said. They exchanged a few more words and Pap and I left.

Half a block from the hotel Pap showed me the money, which was all the change from the $100 that she had let him keep for just running that errand. Almost $80 "Keeping this lady happy has provided us with the extra money we need. No need telling Mam about seeing her naked." I got the drift quickly. Pap said she had two children, a daughter Nellie, four years older than I and a son my sister's age. She had been married to an American and her older son had died in the war. Therefore she received money every month from the American Government and with the exchange into guldens that was a rich living for her in Holland.

Pap came home two or three times a week with extra food and money. I never went with him again, but that naked Susanna image made me think a lot. What other errands did Pap do?

CHAPTER 34

LAST CHAPTER

Pap was pacing up and down the living room through the dining room. A quick turn around by the window and back again. Something was brewing in that small head of his!

No use asking questions at this stage; he would talk when he was good and ready. This time it took weeks before he was ready to talk. In fact one day I found myself starting to pace up and down wondering if it would help my thinking process and it did! A quick glance out the window before turning seemed to give a breath of fresh air to my thoughts.

On Saturday we had one of our family special lunches. I loved those lunches because there was always something special presented and we were allowed to take turns to say what we thought.

It also gave me a chance to show how stupid my sister was by beating her to the punch with questions and answers. But Pap would put a quick stop to that. Else did not know or understand anything about important things. Her important things were dresses, shoes, her hair and getting me in trouble.

During the last special family lunch Mam announced she was having another baby. First I did not care, but later I had to help a lot and therefore was more involved. Silently I hoped it would be another boy; one sister is all I could handle. When it turned out to be a boy I knew someone rewarded me for all the work I did.

At this special lunch, I tried to guess by watching Pap if it would be good or bad news, but he was a master in keeping a secret.

The table was set. There was steamed eel with mustard sauce, fresh baked bread, fresh bulk butter and plenty of milk, even a glass with lilacs.

It was so silent I could hardly stand it. I was the first one to sit down at the table at my regular spot, hoping they would hurry. After Mam put the baby in the high chair she started dishing up. Always the little ones first, then my sister, then the rest of us. But no one spoke a word.

Pap had to say something sooner or later! I looked at my sister across the table. She did not even know what was going on! Lunches, even special lunches, were not important to her: she hated food.

Pap was hungry. He took several bites of eel and bread. With a deep breath and with food in his mouth he started: "Mam and I have been talking a lot the last couple of weeks. We are making plans to go to America. It will take a lot more planning, work and patience but I think we can do it. The future for you children does not look good here. Especially the boys.

"You need education and I need work, not the work I have now but the work I was schooled to do. With one arm I will always be an invalid in this country; in America I can work and be equal to others.

"Maybe that country and its people will appreciate what I have to offer. I am bringing four healthy children. I think we can do it. The church organization that our friends John and Renee Teague in Nashville belong to will help us find a sponsor and work."

I just sat there as stupid as my sister. No questions, no comments. Usually I tried to be the first one to ask something to let them know I was the oldest and the smartest, but my brain had too much information to digest.

Is this really going to happen? Pap was still talking but it went too fast for me. I was going to be 12 years old soon, I had started grade two in the Montessori High School. Everybody said I was smart, but this news made my brain numb.

After lunch I sat down on the arm of the chair.

It took a long seven years from applying at the Embassy in Rotterdam to actually leaving to emigrate to America in June 1957.

The chair and the corner where the chair was located did not go with me across the ocean. But wherever I am I have my own little corner.

www.ingramcontent.com/pod-product-compliance
Lightning Source LLC
LaVergne TN
LVHW061222060426
835509LV00012B/1388